The Inner Child and Relationships

BUILDING HEALTHIER CONNECTIONS THROUGH SELF-UNDERSTANDING

ELLIE BLOOM

Copyright © 2024 by Ellie Bloom

All rights reserved.

No portion of this book may be reproduced in any form without written permission from the publisher or author, except as permitted by U.S. copyright law.

Contents

1. Introduction — 1
2. The Inner Child Defined — 7
3. The Impact of Childhood Experiences — 21
4. Recognizing Your Inner Child — 33
5. Patterns and Pitfalls — 45
6. Communication and the Inner Child — 59
7. Boundaries and the Inner Child — 68
8. Embracing Your Inner Child — 78
9. Transformative Self-Parenting — 85
10. Overcoming Resistance and Setbacks — 93
11. Building Healthier Relationships — 100
12. The Role of Forgiveness — 109
13. Personal Growth — 119
14. Affirmations — 130

15. Conclusion   137

Introduction

Within each of us resides an inner child - that part of ourselves that holds our childhood memories, experiences, emotions, hopes, and fears. Though we grow bigger on the outside, a precious, vulnerable part remains frozen in time. Getting to know, understand, and heal this inner child is essential for healthy adult relationships.

As children, our self-esteem, patterns of relating, and models for intimacy develop. Painful childhood experiences like neglect, criticism, trauma, or loss can cause emotional wounds within our inner child. Even subtle yet consistent messages that we were too much, not enough, or unlovable can shape our inner self-concept. As adults, when these inner children get triggered, they can sabotage our connections through outbursts, withdrawal, or unhealthy relational patterns. By understanding, validating, and reparenting our inner child, we can transform even the most painful relationship struggles.

Jenny always felt anxious and afraid of abandonment, unable to deeply trust others. By exploring her childhood, she uncovered how her father left suddenly when she was seven. Her inner child held core beliefs that "people always leave" and "I'm unlovable." This manifested in clingy, people-pleasing behavior that pushed partners away. Through visualizations, she nurtured her inner child, providing the stable comfort she lacked growing up. She was then able to set boundaries, communicate needs, and build secure connections where she felt safe.

Like Jenny, self-understanding allows us to trace current struggles back to formative roots. By attending to these emotional wounds psychologically and spiritually, we receive the inner child's unfulfilled needs for comfort, attunement, validation, and mirroring of their precious selves. This heals past hurts that, when left unchecked, bombard our present experiences with doubt, fears of engulfment or abandonment, walls of self-protection, or outsize reactions rooted in old pain.

The inner child also holds our natural spontaneity, aliveness, curiosity, and capacity for joy - traits often diminished through conditioned coping strategies that later limit intimacy. Reconnecting to this innocent part of ourselves makes relationships more playful and authentic. We act less from other's expectations and more from inner truth. This allows for vulnerability and interdependence with loved ones - not reliance on them to fill emotional holes or soothe old wounds.

Through relating with compassion to ourselves and our inner child, self-acceptance grows, lessening projections about not being 'enough' for others. We take less personally, react less intensely, and become more attuned to a partner's own inner child wounds, driving behaviors that may have felt hurtful or confusing before. This builds empathy, deep caretaking, and positive communication.

THE INNER CHILD AND RELATIONSHIPS

There are many ways to nurture your inner child - through visualization, writing letters of understanding, talking to them inside, surrounding them with loving spiritual light, or even playing as you once did growing up. By attending to their needs a little each day, you'll find negative behaviors, fears, and beliefs shifting. Slowly build a healthier inner foundation from which to act, communicate, and build relationships.

The inner child journey has repeatedly shown itself as a powerful path to interpersonal happiness. Bob, stuck in a cycle of failed relationships, always seemed to "love too much" at first before everything fell painfully apart months later. By exploring his inner child's longing and fantasies around love, he uncovered a desire to recreate a nurturing bond never fully experienced with emotionally absent parents.

This painted his adult relationships in an idealized hue, projecting soulmate-like expectations onto partners, inspiring intense closeness followed by crises when his fantasy departed from reality. Instead of envisioning his inner child cradled in divine light, Bob found the unconditional nurturance he had sought externally. Feelings of being loveable arose organically rather than desperately chased in relationships. He could enjoy healthy bonds growing in their own time, focusing on consistent caretaking rather than dramatic highs and lows.

Like Bob, when we approach relationships with innocent expectations, needing another to prove our worth, soothe our every hurt, or fulfill every unmet need, we put unrealistic pressure on the bond. If partners fall short of projections, are imperfect, or make mistakes as all humans do, our entire reality shatters. This triggers the inner child's core wounds, setting relationships up for turmoil.

By contrast, when we nurture the inner child directly, we receive the acceptance, attunement, and mirroring needed internally. Our worth becomes self-sourced rather than contingent on validation from others. When disappointment inevitably arises, emotional regulation stays intact, allowing issues to be discussed calmly. We take less personally, extending grace to loved one's own inner child wounds. This empowers consistently emotionally available, sensitive caretaking that makes relationships blossom.

By relating to your inner child with empathy, forgiveness, and compassion, you plant seeds of self-love that organically bloom, filling once desolate places. Feel your defensive strategies relax; your negative perspectives shift; your reactions soften as unconditional worth fills your being. You open into the present, released from past pain's grip. From here, conscious relationships based on choice rather than wounded reaction unfold.

The people-pleasing fawn type finds the voice to communicate needs without fearing the loss of a relationship. The withdrawn, dismissive type reconnects to buried feelings, learning to be vulnerable and trusting. The inner critic's relentless judgment ceases, quieted to allow gentleness towards self and others to emerge. Such is the inner child's alchemy - transforming relationship dynamics at their root.

While counseling helps many couples, without inner child understanding, wounds beneath surface arguments or disconnect persist, blocking enduring harmony. By committing to daily check-ins, listening without judgment to your inner child's feelings, and meeting their needs - even amidst the churn of daily responsibilities - you plant the seeds for relationships rooted in conscious love to flower.

There are many simple practices integrating the inner child into daily life. Speak encouraging words into the mirror each morning. Wrap your arms around yourself in an embrace when stressed. Imagine your inner child seated beside you in difficult conversations with partners or friends. Consider their reactions and feelings, then respond accordingly. Use visualizations to provide missing emotional nutrients, like envisioning being rocked gently or feeling the warm sun on the skin.

When bigger feelings get triggered, name them out loud - "I am feeling really scared right now" - to soothe your inner child. Or have an imaginary dialogue: "I know this is bringing up a lot of anger, and I'm here for you." By extending empathy first to ourselves, we can better do so for others. Through consistent relating with compassion, neural pathways entrenched from childhood begin to loosen, reforming around self-care, emotional regulation, and interdependence - creating an inner source of relational happiness.

While connecting to your inner child may feel frivolous amidst adulthood's pressures, consider their influence. Unaddressed wounds manifest in struggles with career, finances, body image, addictions, and relationships - originating from places within us that simply ache to be seen. By reparenting with care and understanding, we alter personal narratives from "I am so flawed and unwanted" to "I am enough just as I am."

This changes life trajectories. Long-held dreams that were once abandoned seem reachable. Healthy boundaries become possible. Old relational habits shift - not through effort alone but organically from inner security. You act not from places of need or fear but from wholeness. Insecurities, clinginess, or emotional volatility begin to settle. Positive habits strengthen through compassion's reinforcing nature rather than criticism's draining one. Life flourishes from the inside out.

So relate to your inner child daily. Notice emotions arising without judgment, listening to discern their origins and meet underlying needs. Be patient with parts still hurting, cradling them in forgiveness and love until they heal. Share your journey with trusted friends and partners, allowing vulnerability and interdependence. See how self-care ripples outward, gracing all relationships.

The inner child lives within all of us, impacting how we operate more than we realize. Attend gently to their sometimes buried wounds and watch as if, by magic, patterns that once limited happiness shift. Feel yourself filled with a compassion that extends naturally to friends, partners, and family. Negative cycles transform into healthy relationships. Joy, no longer dampened by past pain, emerges as inner light. And you realize that deep, lasting change begins within.

The Inner Child Defined

Within each of us, no matter our age or stage of life, lives an inner child, harboring all of our earliest experiences, emotions, fears, and dreams. Though we grow bigger on the outside and take on adult responsibilities, an essential, precious part at our core remains frozen at a young age. This inner child fundamentally influences how we operate, behave, and relate - more than most realize. By understanding the psychological basis and impact of the inner child, we gain self-awareness that allows conscious healing and growth.

What is the Inner Child?

The inner child represents the part of us that holds childhood memories, emotional imprints, subconscious beliefs, and access to our natural character before layers of protection are formed. It contains our sensitivity, spontaneity, authenticity, playfulness, and uncensored range of feelings. The inner child's perspective sees the world through a lens of wonder, curiosity, and innocence rather than logic or rationality.

This vulnerable self-formed in our earliest family and social environments through experiences, interactions, and messages absorbed into the subconscious. These influenced the self-concept, relational patterns, coping mechanisms, and beliefs about worthiness that became subconscious blueprints. After painful events like death, illness, bullying, exclusion, or emotional absence, protective strategies layer over the inner child to obscure painful places. Yet this innocent self remains alive under these walls, fundamentally shaping our behaviors, choices, and relationships in mostly unconscious ways.

Psychological Origins

Though first named by psychologists of the humanistic school in the 1960s, C.G. Jung originally described the idea of an eternal child archetype residing within what he called the collective unconscious. This refers to the deeper part of individual psyches containing universal memories, patterns, and symbols inherited from human ancestors over centuries. The inner child represents one of these collective roots passed down over generations through all cultures and mythologies in various forms - like the divine eternal child motifs of I Opera Hinduism or alchemy's puer arteries.

Humanistic psychologists then expanded this concept through increasing recognition that early childhood experiences carry an outsized influence on adult personalities and behaviors. Building on developmental theories like Erik Eriksen's stages of psychosocial growth and Abraham Maslow's hierarchy of needs, they highlighted how crucial it is to get basic needs met in infancy and childhood to establish secure attachment and healthy development. When disruptions like emotional neglect, trauma, or inconsistent nurturance occur early on, a fragmented, unresolved sense of self persists internally and is expressed through struggles like depression, anxiety, and troubled relationships.

By the 1980s and 1990s, the inner child became a focus of the recovery movement, primarily around addiction counseling. Therapists found that beneath even decades of substance abuse lay suppressed memories, unmet needs, and a regressive longing for childhood nurturance never fully provided. Only by understanding and reparenting this inner child could lasting healing and behavior change occur. Codependency recovery further emphasizes how dangerously entwined this childlike self remains with partners and family unless consciously addressed.

Integrative therapists then unified psychological traditions to show how childhood's tender developing self becomes buried but stays alive like a seed needing nurturance to bloom into mature wholeness. Unattended, it manifests through wounds to self-worth, defensive strategies, and reactions rooted in past pain that disrupt adult functioning. Inner child healing - through visualization, writing, dialogue, and journaling - allows clients to meet their own early needs, transforming struggles holistically from within.

So, while the inner child concept has taken various therapeutic forms, at its core, lives a shared understanding that beneath the external adult, an innocent self still exists developmentally arrested by childhood's emotional imprints until consciously addressed. Positive psychology furthers this through studies showing how fostering youth-based traits like awe, appreciation, and curiosity improves well-being by connecting people to meaning, purpose, and an alternative to conditioned, problem-focused thinking.

Together, these traditions illuminate the powerfully enduring and determinative force of our early years that, when brought to light, can shift adult patterns through compassion rather than frustration over their mysterious persistence. By dialoguing with and reparenting the inner child, we extend long-needed empathy, integration, and care.

Subconscious Origins

Beyond formal psychology, spiritual traditions for millennia teach the notion of a soul essence remaining fundamentally childlike regardless of the age of the body and mind. You see this in artist renderings of angels, divine figures like Krishna, Christ, or Buddha surrounded by children, or in prayers that invoke the 'spirit of the eternal child.' Inner child work draws intuitively on the premise that beneath our temporal human lives, an infinite, timeless self abides, complete with original innocence beyond the wounds accrued through living.

Early trauma and chronic stress flood the infant and child's brain with stress hormones that inhibit the full development of the higher, rational functions while hyper-stimulating reactive emotional centers. Unresolved painful memories become locked in the body and limbic area, functioning much like a perpetual alarm system, activating fight-or-flight responses long after events pass. This arrests inner maturation, keeping us out of a survival-based mentality well into adulthood.

Studies in neuroplasticity confirm that the brain stays malleable through life. By establishing new neural pathways through consistent visualization, affirmation, and mindfulness around self-nurturance, regulation, and inner bonding, structural change mirrors these practices. We can establish an inner relationship not defined by childhood conditioning - one built on presence instead of reaction that transforms relational habits from within.

So psychologically and spiritually, we all contain an inner child whose experiences and resulting protective mechanisms greatly determine our behaviors, self-image, emotional availability, relationships, and choice capacity as adults until we lovingly attend to them.

Your Unique Inner Child

Your inner child represents the cumulative emotional imprint laid down before conscious memory by all your experiences with family, community, institutions, and culture combined with inherited generational traumas. No two inner selves are the same, given the diversity of individual childhoods. By tuning inward, you can get a sense of this distinct self who needs your compassion.

Close your eyes and go quiet for a moment, envisioning yourself as a child. What age do you see? Take in their appearance, clothing, hairstyle, and setting. Notice emotional undertones: happiness, sadness, anger, fear, numbness? Allow supportive imagery to surround them. Introduce yourself and ask what they most want or need from you now. Listen without judgment to discern their core feelings and beliefs. Repeat this daily, noticing new layers unfolding over time.

Alternatively, keep an inner child journal. On pages headed with your childhood photo, write letters expressing support, empathy, and encouragement. Imagine receiving this nourishment at the age you felt most emotionally or socially vulnerable. Let layers rise compassionately without censorship or analysis. Creative practices like drawing, collaging vision boards, or singing childhood songs also help access subconscious depths.

Over time, consistent inner-child connection unveils revelations about personal sensitivities, yearnings for nurturance, core wounds, and unique totems - the predominant symbols, images, or recurring dreams reflecting archetypal influences. Exploring your inner landscape unveils purpose, meaning, and catalysts for change that were unrealized before.

No matter your age or stage of life, when you begin, hidden aspects emerge if you relate with patience, care, and forgiveness. Be present, allowing them expression without judgment or censorship. By extending unconditional compassion inward, you break negative patterns and reform neural pathways, awakening parts long frozen in time.

Common Inner Child Wounds

Many shared childhood struggles imprint common inner child wounds or core limiting beliefs that unconsciously drive behaviors and relational choices long into adulthood. These manifest similarly regardless of culture or demographics and can be traced back to formative disruptions like:

1. Emotional neglect and lack of mirroring - Insufficient attunement where parents fail to reflect back loving approval, empathic mirroring, and supportive encouragement can damage self-worth. The inner child absorbs messages like 'You are too much' or 'You are not worthy of attention.' Adults then either suppress emotions and need to lose connection with the inner truth or desperately seek external validation.

2. Authoritarian control or enmeshment - Parents exerting excessive regulation inhibit a sense of autonomy essential for secure identity, self-confidence, and empowered decision-making ability. Later, this fosters resentment, rebellion, or ongoing shame. Partners and friends get perceived as directing behavior versus relating supportively.

3. Trauma and loss - Painful events overwhelm an underdeveloped nervous system. Unprocessed terror, confusion, powerlessness, and grief freeze inner maturation unless adequately witnessed and released. Adults rationalize emotions and isolate versus accessing support.

4. Physical, emotional, or sexual abuse - Blatant mistreatment teaches lessons that people and touch are dangerous, losing trust in relationships and body wisdom. Underlying anger, sadness, and shame manifest through chronic anxiety.

5. Perfectionism - Conditional nurturance based on performance rather than inherent worth breeds criticism, pressure, and emptiness around achievements, leading to burnout, imposter syndrome, and competition, constantly seeking external validation.

6. Harsh discipline - Strict, overreactive punishment fuels fear of failure and judgment from authority figures, including supervisors and

society. Adults defer their own needs and people-pleasing or limit visibility by holding back talents and voices.

7. Addiction modeling - Growing up with substance abuse problems in the home breeds shame and strains relationships, modeling escape versus healthy regulation and self-care. Self-medication continues the cycle.

8. Insecure attachment from inconsistent nurturance - Unreliable caretaking prevents bonding versus engendering secure trust to explore inner and outer worlds freely. Adults demonstrate anxious/avoidant attachment, swinging between desperate clinging onto partners and then pushing them away.

Common Inner Child Coping Strategies

Unaddressed wounds manifest through inner child coping strategies like:

1. Regression - Retreating from adult pressures into fantasy, excessive sleep, isolation, or escapism through addiction or compulsion to avoid pain

2. Avoidance - Disconnecting from emotions completely via repression, denial, dissociation, or projection onto others. Numbness protects yet impedes self-awareness and the ability to intimate

3. Regression - Retreating from adult pressures into fantasy, excessive sleep, isolation, or escapism through addiction or compulsion to avoid pain

4. Compliance - Following rigid rules or internal criticism leads to perfectionism, people-pleasing, and over-functioning, seeking approval yet feeling empty

5. Manipulation - Attempts to control the environment by gaining pity, exhibiting helplessness, using victimization to coerce rescue or dominate through aggression

6. Aggression - Lashing out, antagonism, or bullying others shields vulnerability by channeling anger outward instead of grieving and releasing early wounds

Beneath all these defenses lives deep longing for protection, connection to burdened spirit, and avenues to discharge pain too overwhelming to hold inside anymore.

How The Inner Child Impacts Relationships

Our inner child represents the most tender, authentic part of ourselves exposed down to raw essence before adapting to painful environments through defensive strategies as above. Unaddressed wounds around safety, attachment, esteem, and identity continue influencing behaviors and relationships unconsciously until brought into the present light.

Common themes like enmeshment versus avoidance and desperation versus mistrust manifest through this child-adult filter overlaid onto all bonds - professional connections, friendships, and intimate partnerships alike - until inner origins heal.

Attachment Wounds

Early emotional neglect breeds isolation versus secure bonding ability lifelong. Feeling left unseen, unworthy of love, or connecting only conditionally creates separation, fear, and anxiety. Adults alternate clinginess when afraid of abandonment with putting up walls to avoid engulfment without skills to attach healthily in the long term. Partners get blamed for not providing perfect attunement versus self-care.

Reactivity

When current experiences trigger latent childhood pain - a scolding tone recalls dad's harsh criticism or a friend running late awakens memories of unreliable parents - intense emotions flood consciousness without context unless the inner child integrates. Adults then respond with fight, flight or freeze instincts instead of empowered calm, losing the ability to communicate vulnerabilities, needs, or boundaries when activated.

Loss and Exclusion Fears

Revisiting unresolved grief like childhood divorce or death through adult transitions reactivates panic. So, ending relationships, career changes, or big moves amplify fears of devastation or risk the fantasy of a 'perfect family' again. Partners past and present get burdened with desperately avoiding further loss.

Projection and Displaced Anger

Seeing negative traits like meanness, criticism, or trying to control others defends an innocent self-image by splitting off what feels too toxic internally. Yet denied aspects often operate unconsciously, driving behaviors that manifest through intimate relationships like lashing out or blaming. Partners endure anger arising from childhood source wounds.

Cycles

Growing up with unreliable nurturance breeds anxious attachments, cycling between feeling abandoned, betrayed, or engulfed instead of safe, depending on whether defenses flare towards isolation or merger. Friendships and partnerships suffer whiplash, breaking connections.

Perfectionism

Performance-based self-worth breeds critical inner voices demanding excessive self-control while dismissing emotional needs and limitations. Holding back spontaneous expression strains intimacy. Partners feel the void of authentic relating versus getting impressed by external images.

Fantasy Projection

Early emotional absence can breed fantasized projections of ideal partners meant to fulfill all unmet childhood needs when human reality fails this, rage, resentment, and disappointment repeat the abandonment cycle painfully.

The examples above are just a sample of how profoundly the inner child permeates relational habits until brought into present awareness. By addressing sensitivities, healing wounds, and rewiring neural patterns that were developmentally missed or disrupted originally, more conscious dynamics emerge.

No matter your age or stage of life, understanding and integrating this emotional root system establishes healthy attachment, esteem, and communication, enriching all connections long-term.

Tune into your inner landscape, noticing where child and adult perspectives collide. Do certain relationships or situations reliably activate regressive traits like desperation, avoidance, or brooding? Observe without judgment how freely spontaneous playfulness and self-care arise day-to-day versus constriction habits. Take note of inner critic voices, which are harshest when engaging in intimate expression like creative or sexual embodiment.

Consider the examples above, allowing your inner child to connect current struggles or relational conflicts back to formative wounds without shame. Reparent with empathy and forgiveness, noticing over time conditioned neural nets loosening while new pathways for safety, caretaking, and vulnerability integrate.

From this grounded place, one increasingly relates to all - self, friends, and partners - from empowered choice instead of painful reaction. Notice childhood origins without reacting against them or letting their momentum hijack present connections. Hold past and present simultaneously.

The fruits of inner child healing - enhanced confidence, communication, trust, and liberation - impact every relationship and life endeavor. Their origins lie inward in places tender, powerful, and aching for your compassion.

Chapter 1 Activities

Activity 1: "Mapping Your Inner Child"

Objective: Visualize and identify aspects of your inner child to foster self-awareness.

Instructions:

1. Grab a large sheet of paper and art supplies.

2. Draw a visual representation of your inner child using symbols, images, or metaphors.

3. Label different elements with emotions, memories, or characteristics associated with your inner child.

4. Reflect on your drawing. What insights did the process bring about? Are there recurring themes or patterns?

Activity 2: "Letter to Your Younger Self"

Objective: Create a bridge of understanding and compassion between your present self and your inner child.

Instructions:

1. Write a heartfelt letter to your younger self.

2. Express understanding, love, and support to the child within, acknowledging both positive and challenging experiences.

3. Reflect on how these messages might impact your present life.

4. Optionally, keep the letter as a personal reminder or share parts of it with someone you trust.

Activity 3: "Behavior Patterns Reflection"

Objective: Recognize and understand how your inner child influences your current behavior patterns.

Instructions:

1. Consider a list of common behavior patterns (e.g., avoidance, seeking validation, people-pleasing).

2. Reflect on your own behaviors and identify patterns that resonate with your experiences.

3. Explore potential connections between these patterns and your early childhood experiences.

4. Write a journal about insights gained and consider alternative behaviors that align with your present goals.

As we conclude Chapter 1, these activities serve as your entry points into the exploration of your inner child. By mapping, writing, and reflecting, you begin to uncover the profound influence of your inner child on your life. In the chapters to come, we'll delve deeper into healing strategies and practical tools to nurture and empower your inner child for lasting positive change.

The Impact of Childhood Experiences

Our childhood experiences hold tremendous formative influence in shaping an inner sense of self, relational habits, and lenses for filtering reality that endure unconsciously into adulthood. While trauma and abuse leave obvious wounds, consistent emotional neglect, authoritarian control, abandonment, and conditional approval also carry lasting impacts by instilling core limiting beliefs, arrested emotional development, and defensive posturing.

By bringing empathy and understanding to your inner child's unique sensitivities established early on, you shift from frustration to compassion regarding current struggles. Reparenting developmental gaps with kindness integrates dissociated memories, soothes nervous system activation, and liberates you to create healthier relationships and self-concepts moving forward.

Consider how the examples below echo aspects of your early life experience, noticing where established inner frameworks still operate automatically – and largely unconsciously – directing perceptions, reactions, and relational patterns today so they may consciously heal.

Emotional Neglect

Being raised in households where parents lack skills, bandwidth, or capacity for attuned emotional caretaking leaves children without mirrored validation. When feelings get dismissed or minimized consistently, an insecure attachment dynamic strains bonds, making pleasure and pain amplification in relationships lifelong.

Adults who endured childhood emotional neglect report higher depression, anxiety, and trauma symptoms correlated to deflated self-worth and fears of judgment if openly expressing emotions from overly self-contained habits. Partners then suffer whiplash between emotional absence to sudden flooding or anger when neglected inner depths erupt desperately and then retreat again shamefully.

Consistently denied empathy breeds isolation, advising people to just 'get over it' without processing feelings, leaving sensitivity and social skills undeveloped. This delays maturation by arresting key milestones for security, identity, and resilience. Lingering helplessness furthers rates of chronic health conditions likewise rooted in suppressing emotions and needs versus prevention through early care and communication.

Healing Process

Providing consistent empathic attunement to your inner child through visualization, journaling, and dedicated self-care rituals fosters emotional IQ, developing secure attachment ability. Practice identifying and naming feelings freely without criticism – even seemingly irrational ones – releasing long, unexpressed intensity.

As childhood neglect wounds integrate, notice self-compassion and communication skills enhancing all relationships. Confidently ask for support versus fearing burdening people. See how standing fully in your truth attracts mutually nurturing connections.

Authoritarian Control

Parents exerting excessive regulation – whether strictly religious, culturally oppressive, or militantly perfectionist – breach secure attachment by dismissing child autonomy. Demanding obedience trains outward conformity while breaching inner authority and self-trust.

Adults who grew up dominated this way report struggling with decision paralysis, rebellion through self-sabotage, and victim identity from continuously seeking external saviors. Partners endure the whipsawing between over compliance people pleasing then refusing collaboration defiantly.

When individuality gets criticized rather than strengthened in childhood, self-confidence, and empowered choice capacity suffer into adulthood. Fusing with collectivist ideologies – whether cultural, religious, or familial – displaces personal truth with shoulds, seemingly keeping belonging by aligning forcefully.

Healing Process

Honor your inner child's innocence in the face of authoritarian demands that shame basic needs and self-expression. Imagine surrounding them with unconditional permission to explore identity freely without having to adopt others' expectations.

Practice strengthening inner authority and choice muscle through conscious decision-making around needs, values, and life vision versus default obedience. As excessive external control wounds heal, notice more flexibility and empowerment in relationships with less polarization reactivity.

Perfectionism

Being raised with nurturance selectively provided only when meeting high achievement barometers teaches dangerously that love is earned, not inherent. The inner child absorbs heavy shame around failure and messages they are worthy only through hyper-performance versus being cherished unconditionally.

Adult children of perfectionism report chronic emptiness and burnout from compulsive over-functioning yet never feeling complete. Guilt overbalances positive gains, leading to imposter syndrome, relational masking, and somatic issues around relentless internal pressure disconnected from bodily limits.

When parents conditionally reward external metrics like grades, appearance, popularity, or accomplishments only, self-rejection and self-criticism dominate the inner dialogue, driving a permanent fight against parts deemed imperfect. Adults demonstrate defended competence yet desperately fear exposure of sensitive inadequacy underneath high-functioning presentation.

Partners suffer the void of intimacy and vulnerability never measured or rewarded in childhood. Perfectionists also continually raise relationship bars higher to avoid comfort or calm that risks disappointing through normalized baseline emotionality.

Healing Process

Provide unconditional understanding, appreciation, and encouragement to your inner child regardless of perceived shortcomings. Use visualization to surround them with unconditional worthiness, releasing pressure, shame, and emptiness, replacing toxic metrics.

Practice self-acceptance, including imperfections and limitations, with compassion. Write nurturing letters soothing past failures and current self-criticism. As perfectionism wounds heal, notice more ease, collaboration, and direct communication in relationships versus masking through accomplishments.

Inconsistency and Abandonment

Parents distracted consistently by their own unhealed traumas or life stresses struggle to attach dependably with children left emotionally hungry and touch starved. Being raised by caretakers caught in crises – workaholism, illnesses, addictions, constant moves – breeds insecure attachment oscillating between desperation for connection and avoidance when unavailable yet again.

Adult children of unreliable nurturance report ongoing anxious/avoidant relationship issues manifesting in whiplash intensity. Cycles swing between sudden passionate merging out of separation panic, then retreating insistently, requiring space due to fears of painful engulfment. Partners endure ongoing push/pull dynamics, leaving both sides feeling abandoned, betrayed, or engulfed alternatively.

Early emotional inconsistency also correlates to lowered resilience and constitutional strength since inconsistent attunement prevents bonding hormones like oxytocin from imprinting neural pathways for managing stress effectively through co-regulation.

Healing Process

Offer your inner child consistent comforting connection and empathic mirroring they missed developmentally. Use mindfulness, meditation, nature, and somatic practices to self-regulate nervous system intensities, building resilience and strength.

See how reparenting yourself consistently stabilizes attachment ability in relationships despite lifelong sensitivity to separation. Notice bonds deepening through reliability versus relying on intensity. Practice communicating needs, limits, and choices directly from the centered ground.

As habitual anxiety around abandonment heals through inner security, engage intimacy beyond survival reactions.

Criticism and Blame

Parents unconsciously threatened by children's autonomy and aliveness criticize innocuous self-expression as problematic. Nagging and strictness intend to 'improve' children yet shame their basic needs and intuitive signals.

Life gets filtered through a judgmental lens, eroding confidence. Adults report harsh inner critics driving relentless self-improvement hunger, never feeling worthy unless fixing fundamentally 'flawed' parts in themselves and their partners. Codependency and victimhood increase along with somatic suppression and rebellion, sabotaging joy.

Partners suffer projections of blame, micro-aggressions, and attempts to control through unsolicited advice that dismisses autonomy. Bonds strain under negative perceptions, only seeing surface flaws versus quiet virtues requiring projection healing.

Healing Process

Offer empathy, appreciation, and encouragement to your inner child, replacing constant criticism and correction. Highlight their inherent creative gifts and resilient light versus what parents condemned wrongly.

Practice self-acceptance and compassion to reclaim projection authority inside versus seeking endless external fixes. Notice relationships improving as criticism heals through celebrating mutual autonomy and allowing imperfection.

Trauma and Violation

Sexual, physical, or emotional abuse endured early in life explodes innate safety, leaving devastating imprints of fear and recurring nightmares into adulthood. Survival parts cut off from paralyzing traumatic memories create disconnection and amnesia until circumstances trigger flashbacks reliving original events.

Adults abused as children understandably demonstrate higher rates of post-traumatic stress, addiction issues, somatic pain, eating disorders, and suicide ideation correlated with despair, self-harm, and violent behavior. Trust and body intimacy difficulties challenge relationships through emotional volatility and sexual avoidance or compulsivity.

War zones, witnessing violence, accidents, medical trauma, and natural disasters likewise shatter security for inner child development without adequate support. Resulting in hypervigilance, disassociated identity, and felt powerlessness against larger forces arrest maturity awaiting integrating care.

Healing Process

Establish unconditional trust and safe embodiment for your inner child through patience, play, and somatic tracking versus override. Surround trauma memories with spiritual light to exhume without re-traumatizing through floods of intensity. Shift safety to the present moment through mindfulness versus past or future focus.

Inner child PTSD integration reduces reactive anger, somatic issues, and emotional volatility through nervous system regulation. Notice interpersonal intimacy improving by establishing reliable calm and supportive outlets for residual intensity as past overwhelm heals.

Additional Arresting Impacts

Beyond the primary childhood disruption examples explored above, life losses through caregiver deaths, disabilities, or divorce also carry traumatic impacts on the inner child, given the emotional significance of such foundational bonds before developing coping capacity.

Likewise, chaotic households grappling with untreated caregiver mental illness, narcissism, addiction, or abandonment arrest inner development weighed down by unstable adult problems. The child absorbs erratic instability and mood escalations through their unconditionally bonded psyche, developmentally ill-equipped to filter such intensity from environmental projections.

Discrimination, whether through adopted status, appearance differences, LGBTQ identity awakenings, ethnic exclusion, or abilities, also threatens the inner child's intrinsic sense of connection and belonging throughout communities vital for secure bonding ability long-term.

Understandably, such collective relational and systemic traumatic wounds shape inner self-concept, coping mechanisms, plus automatic defensive postures and projections onto current relationships until connecting scenarios back to root causes compassionately.

Ongoing Healing Process

First, deeply acknowledge areas of childhood suffering your inner child endured that, consciously or unconsciously, still influence your behaviors, choices, sense of safety, and relational patterns today.

Hold this younger self with unconditional gentleness, releasing any lingering frustration over not having 'moved on' or healed their old wounds fully yet. All parts go through the process in their own perfect timing when met without condemnation or constriction.

Open current difficulties in relationships and decision-making to explore potential echoes of past disruption, still actively generating emotions, memories, and beliefs from long ago and still coloring perceptions today. Receive their hurt without resistance or wanting to override its ongoing influence consciously.

Establish safe spaces for your inner child places to release and integrate traumas through somatic release, creative expression, compassionate dialogue, and participation in mutually supportive communities. Consistent inner bonding builds nervous system resilience to endure triggers arising within intimate relationships versus getting hijacked by unconscious reactions.

From here, you increasingly respond to life out of present empowerment instead of the helpless, wounded past, eventually maturing into a fuller capacity for intimacy, communication, and vulnerability, extricating bonds from the cycle of painful projection.

Chapter 2 Activities

Understanding how these early experiences shape our emotional landscape is crucial for healing and growth. In this chapter, we'll explore the intricate connection between childhood events and the development of the inner child. Additionally, we'll identify common wounds that may affect adult relationships.

Activity 1: "Timeline of Emotional Landscapes"

Objective: Create a visual representation of your emotional journey by mapping significant childhood experiences and their impact on your inner child.

Instructions:

1. Use a large sheet of paper to draw a timeline representing your life from childhood to the present.

2. Mark significant events or experiences, both positive and challenging, on the timeline.

3. Connect each event with the corresponding emotions and thoughts you associate with them.

4. Reflect on the patterns that emerge. How have these experiences shaped your emotional landscape and influenced your inner child?

Activity 2: "Identifying Common Wounds"

Objective: Recognize and acknowledge common wounds that may impact adult relationships, fostering self-awareness.

Instructions:

1. Provide a list of common emotional wounds (e.g., abandonment, rejection, neglect).

2. Reflect on your own experiences and identify wounds that resonate with you.

3. Write a journal about how these wounds may have influenced your beliefs about relationships.

4. Consider how these wounds might manifest in your current connections with others.

Activity 3: "Relationship Reflection and Communication"

Objective: Explore how childhood experiences may influence communication patterns in adult relationships.

Instructions:

1. Identify a significant relationship in your life (past or present) that you'd like to reflect upon.

2. Consider how your childhood experiences may have influenced your communication style within this relationship.

3. Write a letter or engage in a conversation (real or imagined) with the other person, expressing your insights and feelings.

4. Reflect on how understanding the impact of childhood experiences can contribute to healthier communication in your relationships.

As we conclude Chapter 2, these activities are designed to deepen your understanding of how childhood experiences shape your inner child and influence your relationships. By engaging in these reflective exercises, you take a significant step towards self-awareness and lay the groundwork for healing. In the upcoming chapters, we'll explore practical strategies to address and transform these influences for positive and lasting change.

Recognizing Your Inner Child

Becoming conscious of your inner child requires mindful inquiry into the spontaneous instincts, emotions, pleasures, and fears arising internally moment-to-moment beyond conditioned patterns of suppression, cynicism, or avoidance that obscure sensitive essence.

Through consistent self-observation and radical self-honesty, you uncover this split-off innocent self still operating covertly from within, looking for avenues to be seen, nurtured, mirrored, accepted, and forgiven for hiding parts deemed unwelcome previously.

Tuning into the inner child deepens self-connection, which is vital for clarifying core priorities, meaning, inspiration, and loving intention towards self and others. From here, more creative purpose, joyful service, and intimacy unfold organically.

Noticing Core Emotions

Start by gently witnessing emotions and sensations running beneath daily activity without reacting, judging, or attempting to override immediate feelings arising. Instead, pause frequently, asking, "What is alive in me right now?"

Simply allow whatever surfaces to be recognized with compassion, not needing to shift or fix anything quite yet. Like a young child filled with candid sensations, receive the full bandwidth of your emotional inner landscape.

What feelings do you want to be expressed? Sadness, anger, longing, frustration, determination, playfulness, anxiety? Allow tears, embodiment, or spontaneous vocalization if called for without worrying about practicality.

Deepening literacy of the psyche's nuanced emotional range builds self-attunement, healthy regulation, empathy, and intuitive wisdom to navigate relationships consciously versus unconsciously reacting.

Identifying Attachment Wounds

Notice where emotional suppression or desperate intensity around others betrays lingering childhood attachment wounds, still actively longing for safety, nurturance, a listening ear, and stable caretaking.

Does interaction with colleagues, friends, or family reliably trigger old abandonment panic or anxious merging demands from unresolved childhood separation? Do public criticism or disappointing results re-expose shame around emotional needs, indicating past neglect?

Once childhood wounds show themselves through adult relationships, consciously provide missing emotional nutrients like gentle understanding, respectful listening, appreciation, or encouragement. Offer the unconditional empathic mirroring needed internally that you unconsciously sought from others externally.

Processing Repressed Pain

Many carry unconscious grief and anger from devastating childhood losses yet to be fully mourned, burdening intimate bonds with unresolved intensity.

Have you internalized guilt or shame around a childhood trauma or death you could not prevent, needing support to process rationally? Do certain rejections or abandonments still haunt feeling too painful to revisit?

Open space to actively grieve past hurts on their own course using somatic release, journaling dialogues, creative expression, and loving community support free of judgment or minimization.

Repressing old wounds delays moving through the natural stages of mourning, arresting inner development while generating depression, resentment, and emotional volatility projected onto unsuspecting partners unfairly.

Compassionately engaging past pain helps discharge intensity that no longer serves present happiness.

Exploring Pleasure and Play

Notice what situations spontaneously activate your inner child's sense of play, creativity, wonder, joy, embodiment, sensuality, inspiration, or peak flow states, losing track of clock time absorbed in the creative flow.

When do you feel most authentically self-expressed, singing, dancing, creating, and exploring passions oblivious to external expectations? Yet then notice inner critics or practical voices that shut these down.

To live joyfully aligned with soul purpose, consistently prioritize activities nurturing aliveness and childlike vitality. Celebrate the sensual delights of movement, touch, laughter, music, storytelling, spontaneity, and frivolity, subverting productivity programming and valuing only measurable gains.

Follow innocent inspiration beyond mental constraints that restrict meaning to narrow definitions. Play awakens inner wisdom and purpose.

Cultivating Imagination and Intuition

Children inhabit magical realms animated by creative imagination beyond consensus reality constraints. They converse with animals, trees, and invisible friends unhindered by materialistic assumptions. Intuition and energy sensitivity flourish before overrides.

Yet stressful environments often reinforce one right way, diminishing creative thought, self-trust, and emotional attunement. Restore these vital pathways through visualizations activating alternate consciousness.

Practice inner child meditations surrounded by wise guides that symbolically heal past wounds. Imagine safe spaces exploring fanciful interests long deemed impractical. Be the mythical hero on an epic quest of self-discovery.

Live imaginatively aligned with soul versus forcing constricted conformity. Let intuitive inner knowing guide choices beyond habitual programming.

Noticing Critical Inner Voices

The mature inner critic develops originally through childhood adaptations to authoritarian forces that demand external conformity, suppressing individuality. Judgmental parents breed an inner judge, attacking self-expression as wrong.

Does your inner voice consistently nitpick appearance, abilities, or creative flow instead of encouraging courageous vulnerability, no matter how imperfect? Are you comfortable expressing spontaneous emotions, admitting tender needs and limitations with partners, or constantly hiding these to appear strong?

Begin witnessing self-directed criticism without believing its assumptions or resisting flow. Then, consciously replace attacks with compassionate understanding about the childhood origin stories generating perpetual self-blame. Send wounds love while establishing boundaries with harsh inner voices.

Releasing the Burden of Responsibility

Many unconsciously carry undue responsibility for events not fully under their control yet internalized as personal failures nonetheless – from life tragedies to relationship losses or career setbacks.

Innocent inner children absorb caretaker problems like divorce, addiction, or financial stress as somehow their fault or obligation to fix, developing chronic issues with guilt, problem-solving other's feelings, or enabling versus healthy detachment.

To consciously release false burdens, create symbolic rituals like writing down past events on paper and then burning them while vocally releasing assumed culpability. Take space from those projecting responsibility onto you to discrete loving boundaries and self-care priorities modeling emotional freedom.

Arrested Self Expression

Unaddressed emotional wounds or authoritarian conditioning often inhibit natural passions and talents from full participation, freezing creative drives to avoid judgment, criticism, or overt attention.

Yet resisting soulful expression breeds depression from the vital life force blocked without flowing channels. Do you often neglect creative or leadership interests, fearing sharing imperfect gifts lacking formal credentials? Does anxiety override public speaking, visibility, or interactions with authority figures suggestive of past shaming?

Building confident self-expression heals fears of unworthiness or criticism as projections from childhood wounds, not truths about actual adequacy now as empowered adults. Release inhibitions through daily journaling, vocal improv, dance, collaborative projects with trusted allies, or forgiving communication with inner critic voices open to revision.

Soothing Emotional Flashbacks

When triggers like conflict, criticism, or disappointments recall painful past memories, learn to first soothe your inner child versus acting out residual feelings onto others repeatedly.

Are you quick to attack loved ones, re-living emotions around past violations before taking pause? Do friends protest walking on eggshells when you grow cold or lash out unexpectedly due to emotional density unconscious even to you?

When big feelings arise suddenly, name them specifically to discharge momentum: "I am feeling intense panic right now about being abandoned yet again…" Breathe compassion to angry or grieving parts so higher wisdom resumes. Reach out for hugs, tears, or rest before engaging people from emotional maturity versus projecting child wounds.

Reclaiming Healthy Pleasure

Many deny themselves basic joys, play, and adventures out of imposed repression that shames harmless pleasures as irresponsible or lazy, thus rebelling through reckless risk or substance abuse.

Or they never developed capacity receiving permissions or modeling to explore optimal intensity levels following conservative restrictions. This breeds disadvantages in tolerating positive excitements like intimacy, success, play, embodiment, or indulgences to balance life pressures. Discover peak flow states immersed in creative passions.

To heal pleasure loss, take yourself on consistent dates for arts immersion, awe-inspiring nature, movement release, creative flow, or soothing touch. Gradually increase self-care adventures as nervous system regulation builds capacity integrating joys long condemned as indulgent or distracting. Reclaim wholeness.

Additional Signs of a Wounded Inner Child:

- Difficulty identifying or expressing emotions openly
- People pleasing and perfectionist over-functioning
- Survives crisis, yet daily living skills struggle
- Fatigue, adrenal burnout, and somatic issues
- Ongoing struggles with self-regulation
- Disproportionate negative self-concept
- Sabotaging happiness or success unconsciously
- Intense magical thinking, worry and future-focus
- Escapism through fantasy, gaming, and addiction
- Blaming others instead of emotional responsibility

The above examples offer opportunities to embrace your inner child with unconditional understanding and support. By meeting their needs consistently mirroring compassion not previously received, you alter neural pathways of safety, caretaking, communication, and healthy attachment that transform anxiety, depression, somatic issues, and relationship struggles holistically.

Daily Inner Child Reflection Questions

What emotions are alive today, wanting expression versus ignoring?

Do I feel safe asking for help and support when stressed?

Am I comfortable asserting needs/boundaries or deferring them people-pleasing?

Do I allow spontaneous play and creative immersion daily?

How freely do I express my full personality with my partners?

Do I take responsibility for meeting my own emotional needs first before giving to others?

Do external criticisms easily derail my self-trust or inner knowing?

Do I indulge in rest when tired or keep overly busy avoiding my feelings?

Do I lovingly encourage my own creative interests and talents?

Ongoing check-ins build self-awareness about unconscious inner child wounds driving behaviors, reactions, or relational struggles arising day-to-day. Meet these needs directly with supportive practices.

Over time, consciously shifting neural patterns around emotional sharing, creative expression, healthy attachment, self-responsibility, and mindful regulation enhances confidence, intimacy, and mutual care with others.

Chapter 3 Activities

Activity 1: "Assess Your Inner Child's Needs"

Objective: Take charge of recognizing your inner child's unique needs through a self-assessment, fostering a deeper understanding.

Instructions:

1. Reflect on fundamental emotional and psychological needs, such as love, validation, and safety.

2. Rate your inner child's needs on a scale from 1 to 10, offering a personal assessment.

3. Dive into reflection, exploring any unmet needs and their potential impact on your daily life.

4. Utilize the assessment as a foundation to develop a personalized plan for addressing these needs.

Activity 2: "Give Your Inner Child a Voice Through Journaling"

Objective: Empower your inner child's self-expression and reflection through journaling prompts.

THE INNER CHILD AND RELATIONSHIPS

Instructions:

1. Engage with journal prompts designed to evoke your inner child's thoughts and feelings (e.g., "What does safety mean to you?").

2. Write freely, allowing your inner child to express himself without judgment.

3. Revisit and expand on these prompts in multiple journaling sessions.

4. Reflect on recurring themes or emotions that emerge, gaining deeper insights into your inner child's needs.

Activity 3: "Visualize and Connect with Your Inner Child"

Objective: Strengthen the connection with your inner child and understand its unique needs through creative visualization.

Instructions:

1. Take control of your mental space by guiding yourself through a relaxation exercise.

2. Visualize your inner child in a safe and nurturing environment, exploring surroundings and emotions.

3. Identify any unmet needs during the visualization process.

4. Journal about the experience afterward, capturing the insights gained and fostering a stronger connection with your inner child.

As we conclude Chapter 3, these activities aim to enhance your ability to recognize and connect with the needs of your inner child. Through self-assessment, journaling, and creative visualization, you're actively fostering a deeper understanding of the emotional landscape within. In the subsequent chapters, we'll build upon these insights, guiding you toward effective strategies to meet and heal the needs of your inner child.

Patterns and Pitfalls

Our inner child's unresolved wounds, conditioned perspectives, and defensive adaptations greatly impact romantic partnership dynamics. Unless brought into the present light, these unconscious forces operate covertly, generating painful relationship patterns like inconsistent intimacy, poor communication, stagnating growth cycles, plus blurred boundaries between past and present experience projection.

By compassionately unpacking childhood origin stories behind current romantic conflicts, you reclaim projection authority from the past, loosening its grip on present relating. From here you respond consciously versus repeating history compulsively through unaware enactments.

Consider below common ways the wounded inner child manifests in intimate relating plus supportive healing practices:

Inconsistent Intimacy

Cycles of passionate intensity followed by periods of avoidance, withdrawal, and rejection often indicate insecure attachment from inconsistent childhood nurturance. One or both partners unconsciously seek the stable bonding missed originally through romantic idealization and merger rather than sustainable caretaking behaviors.

When childhood abandonment resurfaces in present circumstances - like separations for work travel or normal autonomous expressions - it triggers primal panic. The fearful inner child hijacks adult consciousness, desperately grasping for impossible guarantees of eternal fusion to soothe attachment hunger.

In the absence of complete enmeshment, which no healthy relationship can continually provide, devastating feelings of betrayal, rage, or abandonment ensue, projecting wounds from decades earlier onto an unsuspecting partner now. Significant damage gets inflicted before clarity returns, leaving both sides feeling confused, walking on eggshells, and hopeless to satisfy such volatile, insatiable needs long-term.

Healing Process

Through visualizations, supportive therapeutic communities, and mindfulness practices, consciously provide your inner child missing the safety and nurturance directly it desperately seeks through adult relationships.

Shower this innocent part with compassion for enduring inconsistent nurturance originally instead of reacting against their enduring effect currently. Building internal emotional resources fills the void seeking to be completed externally, allowing intimacy to unfold organically rather than anxiously chasing perfect guarantees.

Unhealthy Fantasy Projections

The inner child retains innocent magical purity yet to be tainted by worldly realities. But when trapped unintegrated beneath adult consciousness, it projects fantastical fantasies trying to fulfill all unmet childhood needs finally through imaginary soulmates, lives, and realities that inevitably disappoint.

Adults with arrested development unconsciously expect partners to satisfy every neglected emotional, spiritual, and sexual longing for decades held unconsciously. So, new relationships begin with an intoxicating merger through the mutual projection of dreamt salvation initially.

Yet when human limitations eventually surface, departing from inner fantasies, deep wounds around rejection, betrayal, and inadequacy resurface instead of savoring continuing growth cycles. Self-fulfilling prophecies manifest by attacking bonds once failing fairytales.

Healing Process

Through therapeutic analysis, honest sharing, and creative sublimation, withdraw unconscious desires for partners to redeem unlived dreams or heal every past hurt that no mortal could satisfy. Redirect them safely inward through understanding, nurturing, and forgiving your inner child explicitly.

Fill their abandoned heart so relationships develop interdependently versus fearing disaster without perfect rescue. Sustain reasonable hopes and participate vulnerably, expressing needs and intimacy challenges as they arise through conscious relating skills.

Protected Emotional Walls

Surviving childhood chaos necessitated barricading vulnerability that left emotional needs chronically dismissed, minimized, or shamed unsatisfied. Protective strategies cut spontaneous intimacy expression and Freeze developing skills for deep sharing, empathic listening, and mutual nurturing.

These same barricades endure unconsciously limiting adult relationship communication, likewise fearing burdening others with special needs for quality time, words of affirmation, or loving touch earlier denied consistently. Self-protection mechanisms interfere with risking rejection through forthright intimacy practice. So covert hints and passive aggression strains replace direct sharing and caretaking.

Meanwhile, the partner feels chronically held at arm's length and responsible for unlocking stubborn emotional distance somehow or accepting the aloof status quo long-term. Resentment simmers on both sides, yet fear opens Pandora's box.

Healing Process

Through therapeutic analysis, understand how past survival mechanisms maintain walls today that inhibit reciprocal nurturing abilities. Then, incrementally lower inner protections by showing up consistently and responding sensitively when your partner shares vulnerability. Empathize with the childhood coping strategies they developed for reasonable protection then.

Thank barriers for shielding your original innocence so long at great cost to overall thriving and encourage these parts to relax control, believing it finally safe to risk intimacy. Imagine your inner child guarded yet desperately hungry for affection. Visualize their guarded heart opening to give and receive love intuitively, cultivating safe relating skills together.

Displaced Negative Projections

Unhealed pain unconsciously seeks outlets through misdirected blame, punishment, or attempts to control others instead of grieving losses inwardly. Infantile survival reactions attack the present to ameliorate past helplessness yet destroy relationships in its warpath.

Adults abused, neglected, or abandoned as young children often report higher rates of domestic violence, unconsciously perpetuating generational oppression. Early emotional survival instincts become hair triggered by even mild perceived threats long after real dangers pass.

When present interactions recall painful histories through associated sensory cues - perhaps raised voices during couple conflict evoking dad's alcohol-fueled tirades - flashbacks of previous violations surface without context unless consciously unpacked. Inner child terror, rage, and shame explode through adult conduits, unable to source sensations accurately. Partners endure undisplaced reactions unaware.

Healing Process

Through mindfulness practices, build the capacity to witness big triggering emotions as manifestations of your inner child's justified pain versus proof of current danger. Pause reaction cycles by naming their origin without projecting histories onto here-and-now reality falsely conflated by your survival brain.

Breathe tenderly while explaining intense feelings to partners compassionately. Request supportive hugs and kind understanding for enduring early traumas now needing outlets until fully released through inner child work. Apologize for the misdirected intensity that belongs inwardly, not outwardly.

As past pain integrates freeing survival instincts towards safe embodiment and mutual care, show up consistently trustworthy and communicative through frustrating moments, consciously channeling loving maturity emotionally earned through much dedication practice.

Passive Communication

Authoritarian childhoods inhibited questioning elders directly, while traumatic losses stole voice altogether. Young parts split off from maturing self-concept buried assertive drives and direct intimacy skills beneath chronic social anxiety comorbid with PTSD.

Passive aggressive projections manifest through withdrawal or adherence, signaling dissatisfaction out of fearing the conflicts or abandonment risks of transparent conversations. Hints get dropped through moodiness, sarcasm, and ultimatums that force the other to guess true feelings. Hidden rules expect mind reading. "No" never vocalizes, leaving both unfulfilled.

Healing Process

Through role-playing practice, build emotional muscles for vulnerable self-disclosing using "I statements" free of criticism or defensiveness. Pause reactions noticing passive roots effective earlier yet outgrown now. Thank youthful coping instincts for protective intentions while encouraging flexibility suitable for egalitarian adult relating versus top-down compliance dynamics internalized as home life templates unconsciously.

Visualize your inner child learning to confidently voice feelings and needs. Name limits without fearing loss of love. Request conversations do-overs when falling into indirect patterns. Each effort builds neural pathways for mutual empowerment communication.

Fear of Engulfment

The inner child retains psychic sensitivity and is easily overstimulated by energies and emotions before developed filters arise. Too much togetherness may recall enmeshed family dynamics breaching personal boundaries developmentally.

Closeness gets conflated unconsciously with losing differentiated identity rather than fueling intimacy through voluntary interdependence. Physical and emotional merger activates fears of betraying selfhood through imagined abandonment of individual needs while obeying collectivist directives intuitively associated with affection due to childhood wounding dynamics around love withdrawal when intimacy intensifies, leaving partners feeling suddenly abandoned and wondering what happened without context about inner origin stories.

Healing Process

Through therapeutic analysis, uncover specific sensitivities and triggers behind engulfment fears - perhaps transitions from extended quality time to autonomous activity - wrongly associated with violations of selfhood so they unravel as inaccurate threats.

Develop a nuanced vocabulary of needs for both separation and intimate bonds, communicating these vulnerable spaces directly without blame. Negotiate kindly through natural introvert/extrovert rhythms misunderstood previously through inner child projection.

Imagine telling little ones they remain safe to enjoy nurturing bonds while also taking caring space precisely so further union unfolds organically, not forced. Build capacity slowly, expanding windows for consistent intimacy that avoids hit/run attachment cycles, healing security gradually and relationally.

Repeating Destructive Choices

Early life chaos encoded instincts associating intensity fluctuations with passion, chaotic behaviors with childhood baseline "normal," and mistreatment masquerading unconsciously as true belonging.

So victim/rescuer pairings manifest through ongoing attraction towards narcissists, withholders, and controllers that recreate distressing origin dynamics subconsciously seeking different outcomes. Yet without self-aware clarity, psychodynamics compulsively repeat until ties are painfully severe despite contrary intentions.

Childhood coping strategies endure reactively from these conditioned default frameworks until adverse inner working models become consciously replaced with caring steadiness, reorganizing neural circuitry through consistent healthy relating.

Healing Process

Incrementally disentangle fears, insecurities, and sensations associated with bonding since youth by exposing hidden narratives through daily check-in questions that unravel survival patterns below conscious awareness.

Bring compassionate awareness towards unhealthy compulsions, witnessing hidden motivations without judgment before taking responsibility through asking for outside support, and ending self-destructive relationship cycles.

Through therapy and sharing honestly in supportive communities, replace longtime defensive postures with healthy communication habits that are truly aligned with core needs and wounds constructively so that transformation unfolds organically.

Addictive Tendencies

The inner child retains a limitless longing for unconditional nurturance, affection, recognition, seeing, and sensing fully without restraint. So substance abuse or process addictions temporarily pacify unmet developmental needs before repeatedly exacerbating emptiness when unrealistic fantasies collide with outcomes through obsessive denial and repression.

Ongoing addiction manifests through attachment traumas seeking wholeness externally versus recognizing already the whole essence denied inwardly. Habits provide intensity peaks, satiating separation panic amidst denial lows, perpetuating bargaining for salvation through just one more high falsely promising liberation.

Relationships suffer rollercoasters of erratic emotional needs desperately projected outward then rejected internally through repetitive self-abandonment cycles blocking authentic mutually caring bonds from sustaining consciously.

Healing Process

Slowly release false identities grounded in lack, insufficiency, and relational betrayal through accepting here now abundance grounded in interconnection and sovereign safety. Receive nourishment through body, nature, and creativity without grasping or numbing awareness.

Befriend all emerging sensations and longings inside with unconditional compassion. Welcome waves of grief, hunger, shame, and despair when they arise as opportunities for cracking open further into vulnerable authenticity. Let revelations repattern bonding templates at rhythms digestible through your unique journey.

Keep reaching out for communal reflections of love, unpacking generational patterns layer by layer until clarity returns, renewing commitment to your cherished hopes and highest praying.

Additional Common Patterns:

Feeling compelled to repeatedly fix/save emotionally unavailable partners

Intense jealousy controlling partner's outside connections

Rushing bonding prematurely out of abandonment anxiety

Self-sabotage when relationships become too stable

Ongoing misinterpretations and projections about intent

Retreating emotionally for self-protection at any sign of conflict

Clinging onto painful relationships due to fear of uncertainty

Assuming responsibility for managing partner's emotions/reactions

Essentially, all dynamics colored through a child's fear, emotionality, and magical hopes versus grounded adult relating can be traced back to our inner child's lingering influence, still calling the unconscious shots in intimate relating!

By continually checking in on core fears, wounds, longings, and sensations seeking safe integration through your journey, attachment patterns reformulate based on current fulfillment needs rather than past unattained desires still projected today. Notice childhood origins without reacting against their presence. Hold with compassion. And feel the tension lift from releasing the past's involving grip on today's relationships moment by liberating moment.

Chapter 4 Activities

Understanding the intricate ways your inner child manifests in romantic relationships in these patterns is crucial for cultivating healthy and fulfilling connections.

Activity 1: "Mapping Your Attachment Style"

Objective: Recognize Your Attachment Style in Romantic Relationships

Understand how your attachment style influences your romantic relationships through a self-assessment mapping exercise.

Instructions:

1. Familiarize yourself with different attachment styles (secure, anxious, avoidant).

2. Utilize a self-assessment tool or questionnaire to identify your predominant attachment style.

3. Create a visual map illustrating how your attachment style manifests in past and present romantic relationships.

4. Reflect on how understanding attachment styles contributes to healthier dynamics in your relationships.

Activity 2: "Reflect on Codependency"

Explore and assess codependent tendencies through self-reflection, identifying potential patterns.

Instructions:

1. Examine a list of common codependent behaviors (e.g., excessive caretaking, difficulty setting boundaries).

2. Reflect on your own behaviors, identifying patterns that resonate with your experiences.

3. Engage with journal prompts exploring how these behaviors may relate to your inner child's needs.

4. Brainstorm alternative, healthier responses to these tendencies to foster personal growth.

Activity 3: "Navigate Conflict with Compassion"

Enhance conflict resolution skills by exploring the influence of your inner child on conflict avoidance and developing healthier strategies.

Instructions:

1. Consider a scenario involving conflict in your romantic relationship.

2. Reflect on your typical response to conflict, recognizing any avoidance patterns.

3. Engage with journal prompts to identify triggers related to your inner child's past experiences.

4. Develop proactive strategies for navigating conflict with empathy and open communication, promoting healthier relationship dynamics.

As we conclude Chapter 4, these activities aim to deepen your awareness of how the inner child influences patterns and pitfalls in romantic relationships. By exploring attachment styles, codependency, and conflict avoidance, you're equipped with valuable insights to foster healthier connections. In the upcoming chapters, we'll delve into practical strategies to address and transform these patterns for more fulfilling relationships.

Communication and the Inner Child

Our inner child's core fears, wounds, and resulting adaptive postures greatly impact communication habits in intimate relationships - for better or worse!

Unresolved developmental trauma stemming from inconsistent attachment, emotional neglect, authoritarian control, or conditional worth breeds two common communication struggles in adulthood:

1. Emotional walls and avoidance from deadening vulnerability too painful for young nervous systems to process at the time often endure unconsciously through adulthood, blocking direct sharing around intimacy needs.

2. Raw survival emotions like panic, rage, desperation, or shame beyond mature regulation bleed uncontrolled into present interac-

tions when childhood wounds trigger, causing dramatic relationship volatility.

Unless inner child origins compassionately integrate, allowing authentic, emotionally available communication to unfold, relationships suffer recurring pain cycles limiting conflict resolution, mutual caretaking, and positive progress.

By understanding childhood psychological roots behind ineffective communication patterns plus adopting supportive practices, couples transform core relating templates - no matter how long dysfunctional habits endured previously seeming hopelessly immutable.

Let's explore key inner child healing solutions for common communication complaints:

Speaking Different Love Languages

Childhood emotional needs denied make partners crave distinct expressions of affection. So one may seek words of affirmation and praise due to lack thereof from unaffectionate parents while the other hopes for tangible acts of service never provided consistently amidst household chaos growing up.

Bridge understanding

Share your childhood stories vulnerable, including specific gaps left around Nurturance. Then, compassionately listen to your partner's experiences, noticing formative wounds still affecting preferred intimacy expressions today. Release unhealthy shame around "neediness" by reframing longing as a healthy asserting of natural emotional requirements all humans share for wholesome development.

Next, commit to expressing each other's unmet childhood yearnings deliberately through agreed love languages daily until neural pathways lift baseline feelings of safety, caretaking, and attachment security foreign previously.

Unspoken Rules and Passive Aggression

Strict authoritarian parents prohibit vulnerable self-expression in childhood, forcing repression of authentic feelings and needs, leading to passive aggression and estranged blocks in intimate relating due to a lack of empathy modeling growing up.

Bridge with compassion

Make space compassionately hearing each other's childhood authoritarian wounding around suppressed emotional freedom. Then, reinforce relating with unconditional permission, giving for transparency free of judgment, minimization, or trying to fix problems. Thank wounds for past protection while encouraging directness.

Keep sharing authentically and consistently witnessing emotional revelations in each other without criticism to gradually build confidence and neural pathways for intimacy goals too long blocked from fruition.

Excessive conflict avoidance

Children dependent on adult caregivers for survival are already overwhelmed, and open tensions feel too threatening, jeopardizing a fragile sense of security. So swallowing anger and resentment becomes a necessity, encoding conflict avoidance and emotional dishonesty as unconscious communication habits into adulthood, limiting needs discussions.

Bridge with empathy

Recognize legitimate childhood origins, establishing conflict avoidance as a protective measure given difficult upbringings. Empathize how vulnerability and directness may still feel unsafe if needs historically got dismissed or punished when shared openly. Slowly uplift communication confidence through supportive encouragement.

Use the "I statement" to model self-disclosure, then truly listen without judgment, building the capacity for authentic intimacy over time. Thank avoidance patterns for protecting them and inviting flexibility relevant to egalitarian adult relating now.

Defensiveness and Stonewalling

Babies and children utterly dependent on adult caregivers to meet basic needs of survival cannot chance expressing genuine reactions for risk of attachment loss if overly burdensome or unacceptable feelings get communicated instead of idealized obedience or happiness.

So defensiveness and dissociative numbing arise as unconscious adaptive habits enduring into close relating automatically despite regression back to power imbalanced infantile projections at first signs of emotional vulnerability and intimacy negotiations especially around topics still coded unconsciously as "scary" or "unsafe" hearkening back to childhood origin wounds.

Bridge understanding

Make space for scary emotions to be released safely through somatic movement, journals, artistic expression, or trusted counsel without taking defensiveness personally as an unconscious relic of childhood survival adaptations. Recognize one's precious inner spirit feeling threatened, similar to dependent babyhood, despite cognitive awareness of differentiated adult options and agency today.

Provide unconditional loving presence while sharing vulnerabilities yourself, modeling positive communication skills interdependently. This slowly builds neural pathways for mutual understanding, thus softening lifelong walls patiently through care, not confrontation.

Hypercriticism

Parents themselves wrestling trauma and low self-worth from Their early emotional neglect, authoritarian upbringings, or shaming experiences transfer unconscious self-hatred onto dependents seeking improvement constantly against a barometer of "what perfectionistic image would finally earn me safety and love denied growing up?"

This breeds core shame and relentless self-perfectionism (passed generationally), making adult children default to criticism, avoiding emotional intimacy out of fear, and reawakening a painfully deficient inner self-image each absorbed as personal identity in childhood prior to self-differentiation.

Bridge with compassion

Gently unravel specific childhood origin stories fueling the inner critic through past pain projection. Recognize hypercriticism as a misdirected longing for nurturance; address root wounds rather than attacks, which provides space for mutually empowering communication and unconditional self-acceptance to unfold.

Model healthy relating based on respectful vulnerability exchange. Set boundaries against mistreatment Dimension while compassionately listening to underlying hurts without absorbing harmful behaviors personally. Break intergenerational cycles through security earned slowly by risking imperfect emotional availability until intimacy confidence builds strong.

Additional Common Examples:

- Expressing anger through blame statements instead of vulnerable sharing
- Repeatedly interrupting and talking over partner's perspective
- Withdrawing emotional needs and reactions reflexively
- People pleasing and fawning conflict avoidance
- Saying "fine" when everything feels wrong
- Tiptoeing around intense mood reactivity

Essentially, anytime adult relating regresses unconsciously back to childhood survival mode, communication dynamics suffer arrested development until compassionately addressed.

The inner child's desperate bid for safety freezes adaptive skills developmentally, waiting until consistent, authentic witnessing allows thawed feelings and needs to integrate modern relating abilities slowly but surely with practice.

Activity 1: "Your Inner Child's Communication Style"

Objective: Reflect on your own inner child's communication style and gain insights into how it influences your interactions with your partner.

Instructions:

1. Consider a recent communication scenario with your partner.

2. Reflect on your own communication style during this interaction, considering tone, body language, and choice of words.

3. Write a journal about how your inner child's needs and past experiences may have influenced your communication.

4. Identify one aspect of your communication style that you would like to adjust to better meet your inner child's needs and enhance connection.

Activity 2: "Listening to Your Partner's Inner Child"

Objective:

Enhance your ability to listen and understand your partner's inner child by engaging in reflective exercises.

Instructions:

1. During a calm moment with your partner, discuss the concept of the inner child and its influence on communication.

2. Each partner takes turns sharing a childhood memory that may impact their communication style.

3. Practice active listening without judgment, and reflect on how your partner's inner child may influence their communication.

4. Exchange thoughts and discuss ways to support each other's inner child needs in future conversations.

Activity 3: "Empathetic Communication Role Play"

Objective:

Practice empathetic communication by engaging in a role-play exercise that addresses both partners' inner child needs.

Instructions:

1. Choose a common communication challenge within your relationship.

2. Take turns playing with each other and expressing your feelings, needs, and concerns related to the selected challenge.

3. Practice active listening and responding with empathy, acknowledging each other's inner child needs.

4. Reflect on the experience and discuss how this empathetic communication approach can be applied in real-life scenarios.

By exploring your own communication style, listening to your partner's inner child, and practicing empathetic dialogue, you're actively contributing to a more connected and fulfilling relationship. In the upcoming chapters, we'll continue to explore practical strategies for deeper connection and growth.

Boundaries and the Inner Child

Our inner child's formative experiences greatly influence our ability to set and maintain healthy emotional and physical boundaries in relationships as adults.

Inconsistent nurturance, authoritarian control, perfectionism pressures, criticism, and trauma during childhood development all disrupt secure attachment bonds, leaving a legacy of fear, shame, and struggle around upholding boundaries later on.

When the developing inner child gets overwhelmed by invasive experiences, breaching consent too early without developed coping capacities yet, a sense of violation and loss of trust in the safety of vulnerable spaces endures unconsciously, causing ongoing relationship issues until compassionately addressed.

By raising awareness of boundaries and struggles rooted in childhood wounds, we access empowerment and training opportunities for practicing clarity of consent, need fulfillment, crisis management, and intimacy negotiations through a trauma-informed lens no matter how much time has passed.

It is never too late to integrate self-protective skills, strengthening supportive communities, allowing us to rewrite limiting neural pathways from past pain into healthy attachment templates built slowly but surely through dedication now too conscious relating able to thrive for lifetimes.

Types of Boundaries

The four primary categories of essential boundaries include:

Physical - Protecting bodily safety, privacy, and sexuality

Emotional - Communicating feelings/needs free of repression or aggression

Mental - Honoring perspectives while allowing philosophical autonomy

Spiritual - Upholding personal truth without imposing beliefs

Ideally, these boundaries develop naturally in childhood by parents modeling respect, attunement, and empathy for a growing individual's distinct needs and perspectives while providing age-appropriate scaffolding around emotional skills and sexuality education in the absence of dogma or oppression.

Yet traumatic disruption often requires remedial boundary-building later on through therapeutic support groups, consent education, embodied healing arts, conflict mediation, and ongoing inner child integration practices strengthening resilient relating templates developmentally missed.

Fear of Abandonment

When the inner child experiences conditional nurturance or inconsistent attachment early on, an engrained association with expressing feelings or unmet needs as 'burdensome,' unsafe, or causing a loved one's rejection or abandonment often endures unconsciously into adulthood.

So clear boundaries rooted in authentic communications remain chronically feared as "selfish," unrealistic, or threatening intimate bonds. Adults may tolerate poor caretaking, disrespect, overlapping relationships, or even abuse rather than lose primary intimate bonds altogether by asserting healthy needs directly.

Healing process

Through talk therapy, support groups, and childhood origin inquisition, build conscious awareness around false fears based on past wounds versus current circumstances. Then, incrementally strengthen self-trust with boundary communications, knowing the adult partner (unlike overwhelmed or narcissistic early caregivers) responds empathically without retribution so progress continues, building confidence slowly through reciprocal good faith efforts.

Habitual People Pleasing

The inner child socializes extensively towards obedience and conformity to parental, cultural, or institutional authority figures for the sake of belonging and safety and learns shame and anxiety around expressing preferences, dislikes, or objections - no matter how mildly stated or reasonable - for fear of judgment, punishment or exclusion if disrupting groupthink directives.

This arrests emotional development, establishing repression, indirect communication, and passive aggression as default operating habits into adulthood, allowing ongoing disregard for personal boundaries and needs to be subsumed under people-pleasing habits that continue limiting self-actualization and empowerment unconsciously.

Healing Process

Through therapeutic analysis, gently unravel specific childhood origin stories, establishing automatic people-pleasing habits over personal needs as safe adaptation then while acknowledging essential maturation towards autonomy and self-honoring boundaries today. Develop nuanced emotional language, spontaneous expression practice, and trusting support communities facilitating the vulnerability growing process incrementally without undue self-judgment. Soon, confidence replaces repression, opening up freedoms to relate interdependently.

Perfectionism Pressures

The inner child conditioned that acceptance and rewards intimately entwined with performance metrics around achievement, appearances, popularity, or responsibility absorbed painful lessons that unconditional love remains perpetually out of reach.

Harsh inner critics arose, attacking inevitable mistakes or limitations still haunting intimate bonds with unrelenting expectations projecting unresolved ideals, standards, and frustration that partners now unfairly face as casualties of childhood emotional negation.

This arrests nourishing opportunities for empathic listening, forgiveness, emotional risk-taking, and shared support abundant through committed relationships too often viewed through a perfectionistic lens, blocking experiences of holistic nurturance.

Healing Process

Through meditations, envision the inner child seated beside harsh critics, visualizing their origin stories in early authoritarian emotional climates. Send unconditional love and mirroring to the burdensome standards bearer, forgiving its survival motivations while reclaiming personal authority. Then, write nurturing dialogues expressing appreciation and value for qualities beyond metric measures alone.

Turn towards relationships through generous perspective-taking, reciprocating emotional availability beyond surface roles, and letting go of assumptions of perfect controllability - a childish illusion projected from past to present. Guide bonding through compassion, not compulsion. Soon, positive feedback loops were reflected in mutual thriving.

Self-sabotage and Crisis Creation

The traumatized inner child desperate for absent nurturance, stability, and loving witness not provided adequately during overwhelming situations in childhood developmentally arrests subconsciously recreating intensity and chaos unconsciously through adulthood, seeking to finally resolve and heal past abandonment, neglect, and devastation still awaiting integration.

Until childhood origins unravel with compassion, intimate relationships suffer ongoing cycles of drama, crisis, and push/pull projections from unresolved pain fueling maladaptive mental health and self-sabotaging behaviors seeking healing through connection - yet patterns continually undermine secure attachment bonds forming through repeatedly instigating conflict, dishonesty, triangulation, and refusal to receive loving support once consciously sought out.

Healing Process

Dedicate to mindful self-inquiry, identifying when, where, and how self-sabotaging urges arise triggered by unconscious memories of past uncertainties and grief. Release false responsibility to single-handedly resolve all problems alone. Receive loving witnesses reparenting the once abandoned inner child now.

Embrace healthy interdependence boundaries through consistent mutual caretaking. Apologize for unnecessary intensity projections each time while incrementally exchanging limiting behaviors for grounding practices like meditation, creative expression of shadows, integrated and sober communications, and rebuilding secure trust earned slowly through shared vulnerability and forgiveness.

Disability and Illness

Chronic trauma, inherited disability, or adverse childhood events trigger overwhelming physical and emotional pain exceeding the limited coping capacities of innocent nervous systems ill-equipped to manage harsh realities without consistent loving support.

Excruciating burdens live on through somatic issues, disability management challenges, and mental health crises awaiting comprehensive witnessing and transformative justice long denied due to historical oppression of difference and vulnerability. Inner children carry implicit grief and rage when medical establishments and families of origin perpetuate ableism through dismissal, avoidance, and minimization of sensitive sharing, blocking access to vital healing.

Healing Process

Conduct painstaking inquisition and radical self-honesty, excavating unconscious beliefs entangling worthiness with productivity, independence, or external beauty standards measuring so-called legitimacy for basic rights and access. Release false notions of deserved suffering, burdening loved ones, and belonging only through extraordinary resilience disproving vulnerability.

Receive the inner child's understandable despair and fury compassionately without resistance or spiritual bypass. Surround their precious spirit with fierce advocacy of human and ancestral affirming sacred interconnection beyond reductive deficits-focused labeling. Guide all relations through universal design principles that ensure multidimensional accessibility, expanding supportive care communities' commitment to embracing unique embodiment long denied.

Additional Wounding Origins

Further examples disruptive to boundary development if arising without empathic interventions include:

- Witnessing caretaker substance abuse or violence
- Harsh physical or verbal punishment
- Humiliation tactics manipulating behaviors
- Sexual, physical, or emotional abuse
- Authoritarian cultural conditioning
- Scapegoating, bullying and exclusion
- Religious indoctrination overriding personal authority
- Community betrayal and failures to protect

Essentially, any climate coercive, invasive, manipulative, or unsafe enough during childhood development stages to overwhelm unformed nervous systems with a traumatic threat beyond processing abilities risks encoding unconscious beliefs that self-protective boundaries seem hopeless, selfish, or threatening to intimate bonds later on until compassionately addressed.

Chapter 6 Activities

Activity 1: "Reflecting on Your Boundary Landscape"

Objective: Gain insights into your current boundary landscape by reflecting on personal experiences and identifying areas for growth.

Instructions:

1. Take a moment to consider recent situations where you felt your boundaries were challenged or crossed.

2. Write a journal about these experiences, including your emotional responses, thoughts, and any resulting impact on your well-being.

3. Reflect on patterns or recurring themes related to your inner child's needs and how they influence your boundary setting.

4. Identify one area where you can strengthen or establish a healthy boundary to better meet your inner child's needs.

Activity 2: "Communicating Boundaries Effectively"

Objective: Practice effective communication of your boundaries with your partner through role-playing scenarios.

Instructions:

1. Choose a common scenario where setting a boundary is necessary for your well-being.

2. Engage in a role-play exercise with your partner, clearly expressing your boundaries using assertive and compassionate language.

3. Switch roles and allow your partner to express their boundaries.

4. Reflect on the experience, discussing how this form of communication can contribute to a more respectful and understanding relationship.

Activity 3: "Boundary Visualization and Affirmation"

Objective: Cultivate a positive mindset towards setting and maintaining boundaries by incorporating visualization and affirmations.

Instructions:

1. Find a quiet space for reflection and relaxation.

2. Close your eyes and visualize yourself confidently setting and maintaining boundaries in different aspects of your life.

3. Create a list of empowering affirmations related to boundaries (e.g., "My boundaries are valid, and I deserve respect.").

4. Incorporate these affirmations into your daily routine, reinforcing a positive mindset around boundaries and your inner child's needs.

By reflecting on your boundary experiences, practicing effective communication, and incorporating visualization and affirmations, you're actively fostering a healthier dynamic that respects and nurtures both you and your partner's inner child. In the upcoming chapters, we'll continue to explore practical strategies for building and maintaining a strong foundation for your relationship.

Embracing Your Inner Child

We all have an inner child that lives within us - that part of ourselves that holds our childhood wounds, traumas, and unmet needs. As adults, we often push down or ignore our inner child, not realizing the profound impact they have on our current emotional landscape. Embracing and understanding your inner child is a critical step in the journey toward wholeness and healing.

To begin, find a quiet space where you can sit comfortably. Close your eyes and take a few deep breaths to relax your body and mind. Bring your awareness to the child that lives within you. How old are they? What do they look like? What is their emotional state? Don't judge whatever arises - simply observe with curiosity and compassion.

You may see a vision of yourself at a particular age or have a feeling sense of this part of you. Your inner child may appear happy or sad, angry or scared. Whatever form they take, recognize that this repre-

THE INNER CHILD AND RELATIONSHIPS

sents unmet needs and repressed aspects of yourself just waiting to be addressed.

Now, visualize yourself nurturing this inner child. Pick them up and hold them close to your heart. Stroke their hair and tell them how much you care. Say aloud: "I am here now. I accept you, just as you are. I will protect you and keep you safe." Feel your heart overflowing with love and acceptance.

Many of us did not receive adequate nurturing as children. We may have been criticized, neglected, or made to feel unworthy. Your inner child carries these wounds and needs your compassion. They act out in unhealthy ways to get your attention.

One effective way to care for this part of yourself is to have a dialog. Speak to your inner child directly:

"I know you feel sad and alone. You wanted more attention and affection. I'm sorry you didn't get that. But I'm here now, and I want to help you heal. Will you let me show you how loved you are?"

Listen inwardly for your inner child's response. They may share more feelings and memories. Receive whatever arises with empathy. Let them know you hear them and will be there to support them from now on. You may want to repeat this practice regularly to build trust.

Writing letters to your inner child can also help give them a voice. Explore questions like:

- What do you need most right now?

- What are you afraid of?

- What makes you happiest?

- What would help you feel safe?

- What do you wish was different about your childhood?

Give your inner child permission to express their authentic emotions without judgment. By acknowledging their pain and providing the care they lacked, you integrate these disowned parts of yourself.

You can also nourish your inner child through loving touch. Place a hand over your heart center and feel the warmth radiating outwards. Or gently rock yourself back and forth as if cradling an infant. Slow, soothing motions calm the nervous system, bringing a sense of safety. Say affirmations like:

- I nurture you with my love.

- I am here for you.

- You are so precious to me.

Use your imagination to fulfill your child's unmet needs in a healthy way. For instance, if they lack physical affection, envision hugs that wrap them in comfort. If they felt unseen, picture recognizing their unique gifts.

Creating an inner child treasure box or memory book can help them feel special. Decorate a box or journal with items just for them: photos of you as a child, comforting quotes, drawings, stickers, or anything that brings joy. These physical representations make your inner child feel acknowledged and valued.

THE INNER CHILD AND RELATIONSHIPS

Inner child work can bring up intense emotions. Anger, sadness, loneliness, and fear may rise to the surface as past wounds emerge. This is part of the healing process. Allow yourself to fully feel and express these feelings through crying, screaming, journaling, or art therapy. Support groups can also provide a safe space for releasing pent-up hurt.

Remember to be patient and non-judgmental with yourself and your inner child. Change takes time. Setbacks are normal. Trust that by consistently showing your inner child compassion, their pain will gradually transform into peace.

Here is a loving/kindness meditation to further nurture your relationship:

Find a comfortable seat, close your eyes, and take a few deep breaths. Bring your awareness to the hurting child within. Silently repeat these phrases, replacing "you" with your own name:

"Little one, I care about you. May you be filled with kindness for yourself."

"Little one, I accept you just as you are, with all your imperfections and vulnerabilities."

"May you know you are worthy of love, even if you feel unlovable."

"I will be here to comfort you when you're feeling scared."

"May you feel safe and protected in this moment."

Take a few more breaths as you continue radiating compassion towards your inner child. Know that they can feel your love. When you're ready, gently open your eyes.

I hope this journey of embracing your inner child has been meaningful so far. By learning to care for our younger, wounded parts, we experience true healing. With nurturing attention, even the most broken places inside us can blossom into wholeness. There is still work ahead, but you've taken a huge step.

Chapter 7 Activities

Activity 1: "Letter of Acknowledgment and Acceptance"

Objective: Initiate the process of acknowledging and accepting your inner child through a heartfelt letter.

Instructions:

1. Take a quiet moment to center yourself and reflect on your inner child's presence.

2. Write a letter directly addressing your inner child. Acknowledge their experiences, emotions, and the impact they have had on your life.

3. Express your acceptance and unconditional love for your inner child, emphasizing your commitment to their well-being.

4. Revisit the letter whenever you need a reminder of your connection with your inner child.

Activity 2: "Guided Inner Child Meditation"

Objective: Engage in a guided meditation to deepen the connection with your inner child and promote emotional healing.

Instructions:

1. Find a comfortable and quiet space to sit or lie down.

2. Close your eyes and take a few deep breaths to relax.

3. Envision a safe and serene space where you can connect with your inner child.

4. Guide yourself through meditation, visualizing the presence of your inner child, offering love, and fostering a sense of security.

5. Reflect on the emotions and sensations experienced during the meditation, journaling any insights gained.

Activity 3: "Inner Child Collage Creation"

Objective: Express your connection with your inner child through a creative and visual medium.

Instructions:

1. Collect magazines, images, and materials for creating a collage.

2. Allow yourself to intuitively choose images that resonate with your inner child's desires, dreams, and emotions.

3. Assemble these images on a canvas or paper, creating a visual representation of your inner child.

4. Reflect on the collage, considering how the chosen images relate to your own experiences and the emotions of your inner child.

Through the letter of acknowledgment, guided meditation, and creative collage creation, you're actively participating in a journey of emotional healing and self-discovery. In the upcoming chapters, we'll continue to explore practical strategies for nurturing and empowering your inner child for lasting positive transformation.

Transformative Self-Parenting

In our journey so far, we've explored connecting with and nurturing your inner child. This was an essential first step in healing childhood wounds. Now, we'll discuss how to take an active role in re-parenting yourself with the compassion you deserve.

Self-parenting means relating to yourself with the same gentleness, understanding, and care you would show a child. It is based on the premise that you have the innate wisdom inside to mother or father yourself in a healthy way.

Many of us unconsciously learn unsupportive patterns from our own upbringings that affect how we treat ourselves - criticism, neglect, control, etc. Self-parenting requires noticing and transforming these destructive habits into what your inner child truly needs.

Start by cultivating self-awareness. What self-talk do you engage in daily? Are you harsh and demanding or gentle and patient with yourself? Observe without judgment.

Simply notice areas where you adhere to old conditioning that no longer serves your well-being. Common problematic behaviors include:

- Perfectionism

- People-pleasing

- Over functioning

- Emotional repression

- Self-shaming

These reflect ingrained beliefs such as:

- I'm only worthy if I'm perfect.

- Others' needs matter more than mine.

- I can only rest when everything is done.

- My feelings don't matter.

- I'm inadequate.

To transform these, employ the same care and understanding you would show a child exhibiting similar behaviors. Talk to yourself as you would a beloved daughter or son learning these limiting beliefs.

THE INNER CHILD AND RELATIONSHIPS

"I know you want to please me by keeping the house spotless, but it's okay to rest when you're tired. You are enough just as you are."

"I understand you feel anxious about making mistakes. You don't need to be perfect for me to love you. I'm here no matter what."

Respond with patience and empathy instead of criticism. Guide yourself Lovingly while respecting your own needs and boundaries. Offer the unconditional acceptance your inner child craves.

Another vital element of self-parenting is nurturing physical needs. Tune into your body's cues. Are you hungry, tired, tense, or in pain? Make self-care a priority, not a luxury.

Eat when hungry. Rest when tired. Take time to move and play. Receive a soothing touch like massage. Dissolve stress with warm baths. Give your body what it asks for without guilt.

Limit behaviors that disregard your well-being, like overwork, poor nutrition, inadequate sleep, or substance abuse. Make health and relaxation true priorities.

In addition to meeting basic needs, find small ways to bring yourself joy each day. Make time for creative expression: art, music, dance. Infuse childlike wonder into ordinary moments. Delight in nature's beauty, enjoy sweets in moderation or splash playfully in a pool.

Surround yourself with items that evoke warmth: cozy furniture, sentimental photographs, and cheerful flowers. Create an environment that feels nurturing. Include objects just for your own amusement.

Schedule regular playtime. Make forts with blankets and finger paint, build with legos, and fly kites at the park. Play nourishes our spirit at any age. Allow yourself to be silly and unproductive.

Cultivating this self-care lays the foundation for deeper transformation. When basic needs are met, you gain energy to parent wounded parts of yourself with greater presence.

A powerful way to integrate self-parenting is to have a daily loving dialog with your inner child. In a journal or quiet space, check in on their emotional state.

"How are you feeling today? What's bothering you?"

Listen internally and offer empathy for whatever arises. Perhaps fear of rejection, despair over a setback, anger about an injustice.

Validate their experience. "I understand this makes you feel sad and defeated. You have a right to be upset."

Provide the support you needed but didn't receive. Reassure them of their worth and your unconditional acceptance. Suggest positive coping strategies rather than acting out. Guide them as a caring, protective figure.

You may encounter resistance as ingrained patterns run deep. Respond gently but consistently. With time and practice, you will internalize this compassionate inner voice and heal your deepest hurts.

Here is one example dialog:

"Good morning, darling one. How did you sleep? I'm here to listen."

"You feel discouraged because your friend canceled plans again. I know how much you were looking forward to it. You start thinking no one wants to spend time with you."

"I understand you feel rejected, and your heart hurts. You wonder if something is wrong with you. I want you to know your worth doesn't depend on others. You are so precious to me. Let's do something fun together today - maybe go to the park or bake cookies. I want to see you smile."

Make this loving exchange part of your self-care routine, like bathing or brushing your teeth. Over time, it will shift ingrained neural pathways, creating new healthy programming.

Visualizations are another powerful re-parenting tool. Picture yourself as an infant, receiving the nurturance you yearned for. Or imagine a wise, compassionate guide embracing you and instilling hope. Envision your mother or father apologizing for their shortcomings and vowing to change.

Let images arise that bring comfort, safety, and joy. Your subconscious mind soaks up these new impressions of being cared for like a flower absorbing the sun.

Re-parenting meditation:

Find a quiet, comfortable place to sit. Take a few deep breaths and relax your body. Picture yourself as a small child of whatever age you feel called to. See their sweet, innocent face gazing back at you.

Now, envision an embodiment of perfect nurturing stepping forward. It may be an angel, spirit guide, compassionate caregiver, or future self. See them kneel down and engulf the child in a warm, enveloping embrace.

Feel their unconditional love surrounding the child. Hear them whispering gentle words of comfort, encouragement, and guidance. Knowing this being offers endless patience, empathy, and support.

Allow this image to shift as needed to bring a deep sense of safety and care. See the child relaxing in the arms of their loving protector. All tension and fear melt away.

When you feel ready, take a few more deep breaths and gently return your awareness to the present, carrying this feeling of nurturance with you. Knowing your capacity to be your own good parent grows each time you practice.

I hope these suggestions give you an expanded toolkit to re-parent yourself with greater wisdom and compassion. Though the process takes dedication, the rewards are lifesaving. By filling your own emotional cup first, you can then shower others with empathy and care.

Know that you have all the strength within to break free from the past and create profound healing. Keep nourishing your inner child, and rise up to joyfully parent yourself the way you always deserved.

Chapter 8 Activities

Activity 1: "Your Compassionate Self-Parenting Plan"

Objective: Develop a personalized self-parenting plan to cultivate self-compassion and provide nurturing care to your inner child.

Instructions:

1. Reflect on situations where your inner child needs compassion and care.

2. Identify specific actions or responses that would provide comfort and support in those moments.

3. Create a list or plan outlining how you can self-parent during challenging times, emphasizing words and actions that promote self-compassion.

4. Implement your self-parenting plan regularly and adapt it as needed, ensuring it remains a supportive guide in times of emotional need.

Activity 2: "Nurturing Self-Compassion Journaling"

Objective: Enhance self-compassion through reflective journaling, fostering a deeper connection with your inner child.

Instructions:

1. Set aside dedicated time for journaling in a quiet and comfortable space.

2. Write about a recent challenging experience or emotion, acknowledging your feelings without judgment.

3. Respond to your own emotions with words of self-compassion, using phrases like "It's okay to feel this way, and I am here for you."

4. Reflect on how this practice impacts your emotional well-being and connection with your inner child.

Activity 3: "Self-Care Compass: Design Your Inner Child's Toolkit"

Objective: Create a personalized self-care toolkit tailored to the needs and preferences of your inner child.

Instructions:

1. Gather materials such as paper, markers, and magazines.

2. Design a self-care compass, dividing it into emotional, physical, mental, and spiritual aspects.

3. Identify activities or practices that resonate with your inner child for each category.

4. Keep the self-care compass visible and regularly choose an activity from each quadrant to prioritize self-nurturing and well-being.

By creating a compassionate self-parenting plan, engaging in nurturing self-compassion journaling, and crafting a personalized self-care compass, you actively contribute to the ongoing healing and empowerment of your inner child. In the upcoming chapters, we'll continue to explore practical strategies for building a foundation of resilience and self-love.

Overcoming Resistance and Setbacks

We've covered many powerful practices for nurturing and integrating your inner child. However, this profound healing process often brings up resistance and setbacks. Know that this is completely normal. Conditioning from childhood runs deep, and transforming it takes time and dedication.

When difficult emotions arise, recognize them as old pain surfacing to be released. Avoid temptations to repress them or cling to old coping mechanisms. Instead, meet whatever emerges with compassion.

Here are some common challenges that may occur:

1. Resistance to feeling emotions: Our psyche protects us from overwhelming feelings. You may instinctively withdraw when vulnerable emotions like anger, hurt, or grief arise. Instead of shutting down, give your inner child permission to freely express themselves. Let the feelings flow through journaling, art, movement therapy, or another outlet without judgment. This clears stagnant emotional energy, allowing deep healing.

2. Impatience: Re-parenting yourself and healing past trauma is an ongoing process. You may get frustrated by setbacks or the slow pace of change. Remember, growth isn't linear. Ups and downs are natural. Rather than criticizing yourself, offer reassurance whenever you feel discouraged. Trust that with consistent practice, you are transforming old neural pathways and awakening your inner wisdom. Patience and self-compassion are key.

3. Self-sabotage: At times, you may unconsciously re-enact patterns like neglecting your needs or abandoning your inner child. Old habits die hard. If you catch yourself backsliding, respond with empathy rather than anger. Ask what your inner child most needs in that moment. Discover what triggered the relapse so you can better anticipate challenges. Then, reassume your role as a nurturing inner parent.

4. Minimizing progress: When healing deep emotional wounds, you may doubt your growth at times. Notice when your inner critic downplays breakthroughs or healing insights as insignificant. Growth often happens gradually without us realizing it. Make a list of all you've accomplished - it adds up! Celebrate each small step. Your inner child feels proud watching you persevere.

5. Clinging to victimhood: Some find identity in past trauma, resisting change. Make space for vulnerability while recognizing you are more than your wounds. Honor the hurt without letting it define you. You have inherent worth beyond any story of damage or dysfunction. When we release victimhood, we reclaim our power to heal.

6. Loneliness: This work can feel isolating, as few understand it. Seek supportive communities, therapists, or groups where you can share openly. Being witnessed and validated reduces shame and inspires hope. If no outlets are available, journal, create art, or talk to yourself internally with compassion. You are never alone.

7. Fear of judgment: Our culture dismisses "inner child" concepts as indulgent or New Agey. But labels don't make your pain less real. You deserve to access any modalities that lead to peace. If unsupportive people don't understand, spend less time with them if possible. Protect and honor your path.

8. Hopelessness: Seeing how much trauma needs healing, you may doubt true transformation is possible. Recall how far you've come already! Healing happens in increments. With a commitment to re-parenting yourself, you build emotional resources over time. Construct new beliefs of hope, security, and worthiness. What you feed grows. Nurture self-trust.

9. Fatigue: Recovering from childhood wounds is exhausting. Make rest, fun, and self-care priorities, not luxuries. Reduce stress where possible. Modify practices if they feel depleting. Look for joy and laughter daily. Let your inner child's playful spirit uplift you. Remind yourself healing brings energy in time. Be patient and pace yourself.

10. Slipping into old dynamics: The pull of familiar patterns is strong. Notice if you fall into relating to yourself the way your parents did. Move from self-blame to curiosity. What feelings fueled their actions? How can you meet your inner child's unmet needs from back then? If possible, talk to the family to better understand and empathize with their humanity. Forgiveness of them and yourself accelerates healing.

By anticipating common challenges, you can address them with wisdom when they arise. Recall your commitment to showing up for your inner child. Their wounds may resist facing the light. Keep gently tending to them anyway. This builds trust and resilience.

See setbacks as opportunities to practice self-parenting skills. Set realistic expectations. Healing childhood traumas takes time, but each effort makes incremental progress. Notice what helps you through hard moments, whether support systems, visualization, or loving self-talk. What has eased suffering in the past? Ensure you regularly integrate such self-care practices. Make nurturing yourself the priority, not a luxury.

If you ever feel disheartened, recall the profound courage it takes to confront your pain. The willingness to face darkness breeds light. Each small breakthrough lays the groundwork for joy. All the effort you've invested so far has shifted your emotional patterns, even if you don't yet see the larger result. Your inner wisdom is awakening, transforming difficult emotions into flowers of empathy and strength. Keep watering their roots.

Here is an encouraging visualization you can use whenever you need reminders of your inherent resilience:

Close your eyes and take a few deep breaths. Picture yourself as a young sapling breaking through the soil. Sunlight tickles your delicate leaves. The world seems huge and unknown.

You encounter harsh weather - pounding rain, scorching heat, bitter cold. Fierce winds whip your fragile branches. You feel overwhelmed.

But something deeper keeps urging you to grow. You reach desperately for the light, thirsty for nurturance. Over time, your roots dig deeper into the earth, grounding you.

You realize you have everything you need inside to become strong. Raindrops glisten like jewels on your leaves. The storms pass. Seasons change.

Years go by. Your trunk grows thick and sturdy. Boughs, once fragile, now spread majestically skyward. You are anchored in your worthiness. Whatever storms come, you bend and adapt - no longer brittle but flexible and resilient. Scars etched into your bark remind you how far you've come.

When you feel ready, bring your awareness back to the present, carrying this sense of your inner strength. You are ancient and wise. Whatever wounds need healing, your roots reach inward to endless sources of renewal. You've survived so much already. Keep growing.

I hope these tips help you skillfully navigate the ups and downs of profound emotional healing. Be proud of yourself for undertaking this sacred work. Therein lies your light, your freedom, and your peace.

Chapter 9 Activities

Activity 1: "Obstacle Awareness and Reflection"

Objective: Increase self-awareness by identifying and reflecting on specific challenges you've encountered in your inner child healing journey.

Instructions:

1. Take a moment to reflect on any recent challenges or setbacks in your healing process.

2. Journal about these obstacles, exploring the emotions, thoughts, and triggers associated with them.

3. Identify patterns or commonalities in the challenges you've faced.

4. Reflect on what support or resources you might need to overcome these obstacles in the future.

Activity 2: "Resilience Affirmations"

Objective: Cultivate resilience and a positive mindset through affirmations tailored to overcoming setbacks.

Instructions:

1. Create a list of affirmations focusing on resilience, persistence, and self-compassion.

2. Choose specific affirmations that resonate with the challenges you've encountered.

3. Repeat these affirmations regularly, especially during moments of difficulty.

4. Reflect on how incorporating resilience affirmations impacts your mindset and approach to setbacks.

Activity 3: "Setback Survival Plan"

Objective: Develop a personalized plan to navigate setbacks effectively and maintain progress in your healing journey.

Instructions:

1. Reflect on the lessons learned from past setbacks and challenges.

2. Create a setback survival plan that outlines specific actions and strategies to implement during difficult times.

3. Identify external support systems or resources that can assist you in overcoming setbacks.

4. Regularly revisit and adjust your setback survival plan to ensure it remains relevant and supportive.

By increasing awareness, cultivating resilience affirmations, and developing a personalized setback survival plan, you actively engage in the process of overcoming challenges and maintaining progress. In the forthcoming chapters, we'll continue to explore practical strategies for resilience and sustained growth.

Building Healthier Relationships

We've explored deeply meaningful practices to embrace and nurture your inner child. This enables you to transform unhealthy emotional patterns stemming from childhood. Now, we'll discuss how to translate your inner work into building more conscious, fulfilling relationships.

Healing the inner child doesn't end when you close this book. On the contrary, it must become an ongoing lifework. Here are some ways to integrate a nurturing mindset into your daily life:

Commit to self-care rituals that honor your inner child's needs. Make time for play, creativity, movement, and rest - not just as indulgences but as essentials. Set boundaries around work and obligations. Listen to your body's signals. Eat, sleep, and express emotions freely. Discover which activities help you feel safe, joyous, and embodied. Then, prioritize them as your responsibilities, not luxuries.

Check-in regularly with your inner child. Make it a consistent practice, like exercising or brushing your teeth. Set reminders on your phone/calendar. Ask: How are you feeling today? What do you need? What would help you feel happy and supported?

Tune into their emotional state and meet it with wisdom and compassion. If fear, anxiety, or anger arise, embrace these feelings as signals for where more healing is needed. Respond with empathy, validation, and guidance. Reinforce your child's worth and your commitment to their wellbeing.

Intervene when you catch yourself relating to your inner child harshly. Shift from scolding to encouraging. If you make a mistake, forgive yourself quickly, as you would a youngster stumbling as they learn. Protect your inner child fiercely, never reverting back to old shaming habits.

Make your home environment feel safe and comforting. Surround yourself with items like soft blankets, sentimental photos, inspirational quotes, candles, or anything that nurtures your soul. Let your living space reflect the beauty within you.

Find supportive communities to reduce isolation in this work. Join groups focused on inner child healing, mindful relating, or trauma recovery. If available locally, choose in-person spaces where you can receive empathetic witnessing. Online groups also offer connection. Share your journey with others who understand.

Express creativity and playfulness daily. Arts, crafts, music, dance, poetry, and time outdoors nourish our spirit. Allow yourself to be silly, awkward, and unproductive - exactly as kids do! Schedule playdates with adventurous friends. Seek out new experiences that evoke a sense of wonder and joy.

Spend time around children. Volunteer with youth organizations. Attend playgrounds, concerts, or events geared toward families. When possible, cultivate close bonds with loved ones' kids through visits, outings, and activities. Let their innocence, honesty, and imagination inspire you.

Be selective about who you spend time with. Limit interactions with judgmental or toxic people. Surround yourself with those who celebrate and support your growth. Distance from naysayers preserves your energy for self-healing.

Practice mindfulness in daily activities like cooking, walking, and household chores. Bring present-moment awareness to your senses - sights, sounds, tastes, smells. Notice the beauty in ordinary moments. Waiting in line or driving becomes meditative.

Forgive past hurts as you are able. Write letters to family members or your younger self. Speak your truth without expectation. Offer empathy for their humanity. Processing the past from a space of understanding and maturity accelerates your healing.

Of course, nurturing your inner child profoundly influences your relationships with others. Here's how carrying this mindset into your connections cultivates more conscious relating:

You become skilled in empathy and deep listening. Rather than giving advice or problem-solving, you offer validation. "I understand this feels really scary for you right now. I'm here."

Your increased self-awareness helps you choose compatible partners. Knowing your needs and wounds, you seek mates with complementary strengths. You assert boundaries sooner when fundamental values differ.

You parent your own children with more wisdom and patience. Breaking destructive familial cycles, you provide the nurturance you lack. Your relationship becomes one of mutual caring.

You express emotions skillfully. You share neither repressing nor dumping feelings authentically while self-soothing. This invites intimacy and reciprocal vulnerability.

Your standards rise for how you are treated. You cut negative people from your life. Healthy relating becomes your new normal, not an impossible ideal.

You take personal responsibility rather than playing the victim or blaming others. You work through feelings versus acting out. This inspires your mates to self-reflect rather than defend.

You speak up directly when you feel dismissed, attacked, or unappreciated. Instead of passive aggression or silencing your needs, you honor your inner child's worth.

You stop abandoning yourself to please a partner. Self-care is non-negotiable. You model healthy relating for the children in your life through steadfast self-love.

You release the need to control others. Allowing autonomy fosters security - the opposite of what you learned. People feel free to be themselves, bringing out their best.

You no longer accept one-sided relationships. Reciprocation becomes mandatory - shared power, empathy, effort, and joy. You welcome love while protecting your inner child.

When conflicts inevitably arise, you approach them with openness, respect, and accountability for your own actions. Taking the high road defuses reactivity and brings mutual understanding.

You let go of anger and resentment towards past partners. Forgiveness isn't condoning wrongs but releasing what no longer serves your growth. Your inner light builds as you stop playing old stories on repeat.

You become a safe space for others' vulnerability and transformation. Sharing your healing journey invites reciprocity. Your relationships shift from superficial to intimate soul connections.

In relating consciously, you break the intergenerational transmission of trauma. Children see your self-awareness and eat what you feed. The cycles of family pain permanently shift course with your courage.

Here are some real-life examples of how inner child work can heal relationships:

Susan grew up with emotionally unavailable parents focused on work and social standing. She internalized massive shame around her needs. As an adult, she attracted narcissistic partners who exploited her lack of boundaries and selfishly drained her energy.

Through inner child healing, Susan realized she had been subconsciously recreating her toxic childhood dynamics. She learned to set limits and prioritize self-care. Eventually, Susan found a giving, conscious partner who cherished her completely. Her wounded inner child finally felt seen.

James endured physical abuse and constant criticism from his father growing up. In adulthood, he reacted to stress by lashing out at loved ones verbally. His wife frequently threatened divorce unless he got therapy.

Through support groups, meditation, and inner child work, James unpacked his unresolved anger. He discovered self-soothing tools to prevent taking frustrations out on others. Re-parenting himself with compassion transformed his relationships.

Robin grew up bullied for her appearance and shy nature. She internalized deep unworthiness and closed her heart for protection. As an adult, she isolated herself socially and pushed away anyone who tried to get close emotionally.

Once Robin embraced her inner child, she could extend the kindness she'd always craved. She joined groups for social anxiety and practiced vulnerability through sharing poetry. Over time, her self-esteem grew, and she built a supportive community.

Diego was raised in a volatile home with addicts who raged unpredictably. He struggled to trust anyone, always assuming he'd be abandoned eventually. He resorted to dishonesty to avoid confrontations.

Through talk therapy and 12-step programs, Diego unpacked his traumatic past. As he nursed his wounded inner child, his anxiety settled. He learned to communicate assertively and found the courage to engage in intimate relationships.

Melanie's parents divorced bitterly when she was nine. She grew up quickly, suppressing her feelings and needs. As an adult, she became rigidly self-reliant and emotionally distant in relationships. Underneath festered deep loneliness.

Once Melanie embraced her inner child, she realized why she had closed her heart. She allowed herself to be vulnerable, ask for help, and share her authentic emotions. Her marriage grew more genuine and fulfilling.

Jake endured neglect and emotional manipulation growing up. He attracted partners who gaslit and took advantage of him financially. He constantly second-guessed his own reality and needs.

Through somatic therapy, Jake unraveled his family's narcissistic patterns. He nurtured his inner child's buried emotions, learning to honor his perceptions and stand up for himself. The domestic abuse ended as he built his self-worth.

Hopefully, these examples offer encouragement that inner child work profoundly heals relationships. Your vulnerable younger self awaits your compassion. By loving them unconditionally, you plant seeds of fulfillment for your present-day connections to blossom.

Chapter 10 Activities

Activity 1: "Your Relationship Blueprint"

Objective: Create a personalized blueprint for healthier relationships by integrating lessons from your inner child healing journey.

Instructions:

1. Reflect on key insights gained from your inner child healing process.

2. Identify specific behaviors, communication styles, or patterns you'd like to enhance or transform in your relationships.

3. Create a visual or written blueprint outlining actionable steps for fostering healthier connections.

4. Regularly revisit and adapt your relationship blueprint as you continue to grow and evolve.

Activity 2: "Shared Growth Reflection"

Objective: Reflect on and celebrate shared growth in relationships through storytelling and case studies.

Instructions:

1. Collect success stories or case studies of individuals who have applied inner child healing principles to their relationships.

2. Reflect on these stories, identifying common themes, challenges, and transformational moments.

3. Share your own success stories or instances of growth within your relationships.

4. Discuss and brainstorm with friends or a support group how these shared stories can inspire positive change in your own relationships.

Activity 3: "Empathy Building Exercise"

Objective: Strengthen empathy within your relationships by engaging in an interactive exercise.

Instructions:

1. Choose a relationship in your life that you want to enhance through increased empathy.

2. Engage in active listening with the intention of understanding the other person's perspective.

3. Share your own experiences, guided by the lessons learned from your inner child healing journey.

4. Reflect on the exchange and identify ways in which you can continue to foster empathy and understanding in your relationships.

By creating a relationship blueprint, reflecting on shared growth, and actively engaging in empathy-building exercises, you actively contribute to the positive transformation of your connections with others. In the upcoming chapters, we'll continue to explore practical strategies for cultivating and maintaining healthy, thriving relationships.

The Role of Forgiveness

Healing your inner child involves processing immense pain - neglect, criticism, abuse, abandonment. Understandably, you may carry anger and resentment towards those who hurt you. However, holding onto bitterness keeps you trapped in victimhood. Forgiveness is the key that unlocks your capacity to move forward into wholeness.

What blocks us from forgiving?

Pride - We want the other person to apologize and make amends first. We feel they don't deserve forgiveness.

Fear - We worry if we forgive, we are approving or enabling future harm. Forgiveness makes us feel unsafe.

Shame - We think forgiving means the wounds weren't a big deal, or we're somehow to blame.

Attachment - Anger feels empowering. We gain identity from being the victim. Forgiving means surrendering this familiar role.

The desire for vengeance - We want the other person to hurt like we did. Justice equals punishment in our minds.

These are all valid concerns stemming from self-protection. However, unresolved anger breeds more pain. Resentment keeps us trapped in the original offense, unable to move forward. We relive the storyline on repeat, reinforcing victimhood.

Forgiveness doesn't mean condoning harm, forgetting betrayals, or letting toxic people continue hurting you. You can maintain boundaries while releasing anger's grip internally. Forgiveness is for your benefit, to clear heavy emotional baggage so you can heal.

Here are some key mindset shifts for letting go of resentment:

Separate person from behavior - Understand that hurtful actions often stem from the other person's own inner wounds and unconscious conditioning. Their behavior does not define their core being.

Release the need for apology/atonement - Know that you cannot control others' willingness to take accountability. Forgiveness is independent of external validation. It comes from within.

Gain perspective - Recognize most offenses arise from temporary ignorance, not malicious intent. With time and maturity, the other person likely grew in empathy and wisdom.

Find empathy - Connect to the humanity of the person who hurt you. Consider how suffering, insecurity, and unhealed traumas produced their actions. What inner child wounds did they carry?

THE INNER CHILD AND RELATIONSHIPS

Take responsibility for your part - Even if you were clearly the victim, look for any ways you might have contributed to the dynamic unconsciously. Move beyond blame into mutual understanding.

Accept the injustice - Release the need to be proven right or make the other person wrong. Allow life's unfairness and cruelty at times. Your power comes from rising above the story of offense.

Value the lessons - See how the pain shaped you into greater compassion, awareness, and resilience. Find the gifts even in life's hardest moments.

Rest in your worth - Know your value and beauty exist regardless of how anyone treats you. You are inherently whole, not damaged or defined by the past.

Move forward in freedom - Letting go of anger frees you from the repetitive mind loops replaying old hurts. It clears space for new energy to enter.

Here are some tangible steps you can take to cultivate forgiveness:

1. Get support - Find counselors, support groups, and trusted friends. Sharing your story with empathetic listeners reduces shame/isolation. Feel deserving of care.

2. Write it out - Write a journal about your hurt and anger. Articulating the full story brings awareness. Imagine what caused this person's harmful behavior. What pain might they carry?

3. Prayer/meditation - In quiet moments, visualize sending the person (and yourself) lovingkindness. Pray for their inner wounds to be healed and happiness to increase.

4. Self-soothing - When anger arises, practice relaxation techniques - deep breathing, mindfulness, loving touch. Calm your nervous system first before reacting.

5. Separate the person from behavior. If it is safe, lovingly discuss the issues with them. Express your experience while respecting their humanity. Listen generously in return.

6. Set boundaries - You can forgive without further contact if toxicity persists. Protect your peace while wishing them well from afar. Distance can help gain perspective.

7. Perform ritual - Write letters expressing your complete truth, then burn/bury them. Create art as a purging. Hold a ceremony releasing stored anger to transform it.

8. Radical Responsibility - Looking back, can you find any ways you might have contributed, even unintentionally? Take accountability with humility.

9. Turn wounds to wisdom - Share your story to help others going through similar pain. Your compassion can inspire their healing and forgiveness.

10. Core values - Recall shared humanity. What life principles matter to you? Kindness, honesty, service, creativity? Living aligned with your values builds spiritual strength.

11. Therapy/Support groups - If the abuse is traumatizing, find professional help to process it safely. Therapeutic techniques can release anger's grip. You deserve nurturing space.

THE INNER CHILD AND RELATIONSHIPS

12. Self-love - Nourish your inner child through nature, arts, movement, and play. Don't abandon yourself now, as you may have been abandoned then. Stay present through emotional storms.

13. Patience and compassion - Releasing deep resentments takes time and ongoing effort. Setbacks are natural. Keep applying yourself gently. Growth is nonlinear.

14. Higher perspective - Read teachings from spiritual traditions on forgiveness and unconditional love. This lifts the above stories of offense into a framework of interconnection and grace.

15. Model the change - Once you forgive, inspire others struggling with resentment. Your lived example gives them hope they can let go and transform their pain, too.

Here is a simple forgiveness meditation to try:

Sit comfortably with your eyes closed. Breathe deeply and set the intention to forgive. Picture the person who caused you harm. See their human vulnerability beyond actions that hurt you.

Say silently: "What you did caused me great pain, but I know it came from your own unhealed wounds. With compassion for myself and you, I now choose to forgive you completely."

Imagine a golden light entering your heart center, dissolving anger and resentment. Feel your body relax as heavy burdens drop away. You are free of the past story. Send the person wishes of joy, peace, and healing.

Even if emotions like sadness or grief linger, anger dissolves. You reclaim your power in forgiveness. From this centered place, compassion for yourself and them can grow.

I hope these suggestions help you undertake forgiveness as a spiritual practice. While challenging, it is one of the most liberating journeys we can take. By releasing others, we free ourselves. Anger becomes fuel for cultivating fierce compassion. Your light will shine brighter for having sat with the darkness.

Now, we'll explore a specific relationship that often holds much-stored resentment - with our parents or primary caretakers. Healing your inner child involves making peace with those who were entrusted with your nurturance but failed in some way. This requires tremendous courage and vulnerability.

Why is it so hard to forgive our parents?

- The wounds started early when we were fully dependent on them

- Their actions feel like a betrayal of the sacred parent-child bond

- We may still crave their approval and unconditional love

- It means acknowledging their humanity and fallibility

- We have to mourn the childhood we deserved but never received

This intimate family history is painful to revisit. However, taking responsibility for our own anger and hurt allows us to break free. The forgiveness of parents is a cornerstone in inner child healing. Here are some suggestions for having this courageous inner dialog:

1) Separate intention from impact - Consider your parents' circumstances and psychology. Their parenting likely stemmed from generational trauma, pressures to conform, and lack of self-awareness.

Have empathy for their limitations. But also acknowledge the harmful effects of their behavior. Honoring both truths brings peace.

2) Write a letter - Articulate everything you wish you could express to your parents. The full spectrum of emotions - anger, sadness, longing, compassion. Seeing it written out brings clarity. You may choose to share it with them if you feel heard.

3) Grieve what you didn't receive - Allow yourself to feel sorrow for the childhood wounds so those feelings don't get projected as resentment. Cry, create art, journal. Move through the pain to reach acceptance.

4) Forgive yourself - Many feel guilt for harboring anger towards parents. Self-forgiveness allows empathy for them to grow. Your feelings are valid and real. Beating yourself up helps no one.

5) Perspective and maturity - Parents often do their best with the tools and awareness they possess at the time. With age comes wisdom regarding our past and our parents' humanity. Have realistic expectations given the contexts.

6) Freedom comes from within - We cannot control our parents admitting harm or changing. But we can take charge of our inner world by releasing resentment. Don't wait for their apology. Empower yourself.

7) Healing their pain helps - Consider how your parents' own childhoods shaped their wounded patterns. For instance, your mother's criticism may stem from her father's emotional abuse. Have compassion for the hurt inner child inside your parents that they likely still carry.

8) What do you appreciate? Alongside what parents failed at, reflect on what they did well. Did they provide financially despite being emotionally absent? Do mundane acts like cooking favorite meals reveal care in quiet ways? Find the good in them while still acknowledging the grief.

9) Physical distance - In abusive/toxic relationships, maintaining healthy limits is wise alongside inner forgiveness. You can wish parents well from afar while choosing interactions mindfully. Protect your peace.

10) Support and validation - Find empathetic listeners and communities to help you process complex feelings. Therapists can help unravel family traumas. You deserve to feel heard.

Chapter 11 Activities

Activity 1: "Reflective Forgiveness Journaling"

Objective: Initiate the forgiveness process by engaging in reflective journaling to explore and understand emotions associated with past experiences.

Instructions:

1. Choose a specific event or individual from your past that holds emotional weight.

2. Journal about your feelings, thoughts, and reflections regarding this event or person.

3. Identify the impact on your inner child and how forgiveness may contribute to healing.

4. Begin the forgiveness process by writing a letter to yourself or the person involved, expressing your intention to forgive and release.

Activity 2: "Empathy in Action: Compassionate Dialogue"

Objective: Cultivate forgiveness through a guided exercise involving compassionate dialogue with yourself or others.

Instructions:

1. Select a situation or individual that requires forgiveness.

2. Write a letter or engage in a mental dialogue expressing understanding and empathy toward yourself or the person involved.

3. Focus on acknowledging the pain, seeking understanding, and expressing a willingness to forgive.

4. Reflect on the emotional shifts and insights gained through this empathetic dialogue.

Activity 3: "Symbolic Release Ceremony"

Objective: Symbolically release the weight of unforgiveness through a tangible, transformative ceremony.

Instructions:

1. Choose a symbolic representation (e.g., written notes, objects) that represents the forgiveness process for you.

2. Find a serene and private space to perform a release ceremony.

3. Verbally express your intentions to forgive and release the symbolic representation, either by burning, burying, or discarding it.

4. Reflect on the sense of liberation and closure achieved through this symbolic act.

By engaging in reflective forgiveness journaling, compassionate dialogue, and symbolic release ceremonies, you actively contribute to the transformative power of forgiveness. In the upcoming chapters, we'll continue to explore practical strategies for growth, healing, and nurturing lasting, meaningful connections.

Personal Growth

We've now reached the final chapter of our journey together, exploring inner child healing. I hope you feel empowered with new tools to nurture yourself with greater compassion and consciousness. However, the work is never truly complete. Self-awareness and mindful relating remain lifelong endeavors.

What matters most is your commitment to showing up for your inner child consistently. Let this book be a beginning rather than an ending. Growth depends not on perfect mastery but on small, simple steps practiced with dedication over time.

Be proud of how far you've come already. And now, there are endless opportunities ahead for even deeper healing and transformation. Here are some suggestions for continuing to integrate this work into your life:

- Revisit sections of the book that resonate - Flag meaningful passages, tools, and exercises to revisit. Highlight key mantras and affirmations to recall when you feel discouraged.

- Expand your support network - Find therapists, groups, mentors, or communities focused on inner child work, mindful relating, and trauma recovery. We all need mirrors to reflect our blind spots. Don't isolate.

- Look for growth opportunities - Explore workshops, retreats, and training related to your growth. Take risks to gain new skills and perspectives. Take chances on meeting new people who inspire you.

- Make space for reflection - Schedule regular check-ins with yourself through journaling, meditation, and time in nature. Process emotions, insights, and synchronicities. Integrate breakthroughs.

- Focus on one issue at a time - Don't get overwhelmed trying to transform everything at once. Pick one childhood wound to gently unpack. Once you feel a sense of resolution, move to the next.

- Be patient and celebrate small wins - Healing isn't linear, nor is progress measurable. Notice tiny shifts like responding to challenges with less reactivity. Mark milestones.

- Read related books - Dive deeper into themes like mindfulness, nonviolent communication, trauma, codependency, attachment theory, and unconditional love. Keep expanding your knowledge.

- Practice conscious relating skills - Bring presence, empathy, vulnerability, and deep listening to all your relationships. Notice when old patterns get triggered and relate differently.

THE INNER CHILD AND RELATIONSHIPS 121

- Release perfectionism - Progress means being gentler with yourself, not becoming a mythical perfect partner, parent, or person. You are inherently worthy right now in this moment.

- Help others on their path - Share what you learn, either informally or by volunteering/mentoring. Guiding others reminds us of our own tools. Their progress inspires ours.

- Remember your inner wisdom - When doubts arise, recall the profound strength and resilience of your inner child. Trust you have all the answers within. Keep communing with your heart.

- Uphold healthy boundaries - Be mindful of people and situations that deplete you. Limit interactions with those who criticize or invalidate your growth. Protect your energy.

- Build your toolbox - Continue acquiring healthy coping strategies - creative expression, embodiment practices, mindfulness, time in nature, and emotional releases. Have diverse self-nurturing tools on hand for challenging moments.

- Focus on needs, not narratives - When destabilized, get grounded in your body. What do you need at this moment - rest, touch, nourishment, movement? Meet those needs first before over-analyzing stories.

- Forgive setbacks - Growth is nonlinear. Guilt and shame block healing when we stumble. Respond to relapses or backslides with compassion. Begin again where you are. Just come back to presence.

I hope these suggestions offer inspiration to integrate inner child healing as an ongoing practice.

Of course, many other communities and resources can support you on this journey:

- Therapy focused on inner child work, attachment theory, trauma and relationships

- Support groups for codependency, adult children of alcoholics/dysfunctional families, domestic abuse survivors

- Somatic and mind-body therapies like dance, yoga, massage, breathwork

- Nature retreats, wilderness solo experiences, and ecotherapy

- Mindfulness, meditation and internal family systems (IFS)

- Shadow work, men/women's groups, initiation rituals

- Nonviolent communication and compassionate-related training

- Psychedelic-assisted therapy

- Arts/creativity-based healing: music, visual arts, poetry, etc.

Remember, you have all the wisdom within already to nurture your inner child. External resources simply mirror this truth back, reminding you of your inherent perfection.

My deepest hope is that through our time together, you feel empowered to relate to yourself in a radically gentle way. May you carry that openness, empathy, and compassion into all your relationships and moments. Your consciousness strengthens collective consciousness.

This is not a journey you need to walk alone. You are surrounded by fellow travelers awakening into greater wholeness and forgiveness. We are all learning together. Your willingness to face darkness breathes light into this world for us all.

Implementing Lasting Change

For inner child work to truly take root in your life, it is important to set clear goals and integrate new practices into your daily routine. Here are some tips:

- Revisit your journal from the beginning of the book. What did you hope to gain or change through this process? Review your intentions and assess your progress.

- Make a list of insights, breakthroughs, or changes you've experienced so far, no matter how small. This helps solidify new neural pathways and reminds you of your capabilities.

- Note any childhood stories, patterns, or behaviors you would still like to transform through inner child work. Be specific yet patient with yourself.

- Identify 1-2 new practices or tools from the book you found most powerful. Schedule time each day to integrate these, whether journaling, meditation, etc.

- Share your key learnings and intentions with supportive friends or communities. Verbalizing your commitment helps solidify it. Ask for their encouragement.

- Consider ongoing forms of therapeutic support if needed - therapy, support groups, retreats, and classes. You don't have to walk this path alone.

- Set reminders to check in with your inner child at regular intervals - morning and night, certain days each week, etc. Consistency is key.

- When you notice old habits resurfacing, respond with curiosity rather than judgment. Explore when these patterns first formed and what core wounds they reveal. Then, reassume your role as a compassionate inner parent.

- Accept that change is often gradual, with forward and backward steps along the way. Focus on progress over perfection. Meeting yourself with kindness grows self-trust.

- Spend time visualizing your inner child healed and whole. How would they feel, act, and relate to themselves/others? Let this image guide you in making choices aligned with your well-being.

- Research related books, resources, and communities that can support your continued growth. Learning is lifelong. Find inspiration in fellow travelers on this path of self-discovery.

Ongoing Exploration

While this book offered a foundation in inner child work, many other communities and resources can further deepen your journey:

Recommended Books:

- Homecoming: Reclaiming and Healing Your Inner Child by John Bradshaw

- Recovery of Your Inner Child by Lucia Capacchione

- The Wisdom of the Enneagram by Don Richard Riso and Russ Hudson

- The Drama of the Gifted Child by Alice Miller

- Complex PTSD: From Surviving to Thriving by Pete Walker

- The Body Keeps the Score by Bessel van der Kolk

- Attached by Amir Levine and Rachel Heller

Therapeutic Support:

- Somatic therapy

- Internal family systems (IFS)

- Attachment theory-based therapy

- mindfulness and meditation

- Support groups focused on childhood trauma

Body-Based Healing:

- Yoga, dance, martial arts

- Somatic experiencing

- Acupuncture

- Eye movement desensitization and reprocessing (EMDR)

- Ecotherapy - nature connection

- Psychedelic-assisted therapy

Communication and Relationships:

- Nonviolent communication (NVC)

- Compassionate relating skills

- Codependents Anonymous or other 12-step programs

Spiritual Development:

- Studying teachings from wisdom traditions

- Forgiveness practices

- Rituals, shamanic journeys, or rites of passage

- Men's/Women's groups

Chapter 12 Activities

Activity 1: "Personal Growth Vision Board"

Objective: Visualize and manifest your ongoing personal growth journey by creating a vision board.

Instructions:

1. Collect magazines, images, and materials that resonate with your vision for continuous growth.

2. Create a visual collage representing your aspirations, goals, and the qualities you aim to cultivate.

3. Display your vision board in a prominent place to serve as a daily reminder of your commitment to ongoing self-discovery.

4. Regularly update your vision board as your journey evolves and new goals emerge.

Activity 2: "Monthly Reflective Check-Ins"

Objective: Establish a routine for self-reflection and growth by engaging in monthly check-ins.

Instructions:

1. Set aside time each month for a reflective self-check-in session.

2. Write a journal about your experiences, insights, and challenges encountered during the past month.

3. Identify areas where you've seen growth and areas that may need further attention.

4. Use these reflections to set new intentions and goals for the upcoming month, ensuring a continuous and intentional journey of self-discovery.

Activity 3: "Community Connection Project"

Objective: Expand your support network and share your journey by initiating a community connection project.

Instructions:

1. Identify a community or group related to your interests or personal growth goals.

2. Introduce yourself and share a brief overview of your journey, including challenges, successes, and ongoing aspirations.

3. Engage in conversations with community members, offering support and exchanging insights.

4. Reflect on the connections made and consider how community engagement contributes to your ongoing growth.

Resources for Further Exploration:

Online Communities:

- Join forums or groups on platforms like Reddit or Facebook dedicated to personal development and inner child healing.

3. Therapeutic Resources:

- Consider seeking guidance from therapists, counselors, or life coaches specializing in inner child work and personal growth.

4. Courses and Workshops:

- Explore online courses or workshops focused on mindfulness, self-compassion, and inner child healing.

5. Podcasts:

- Listen to podcasts discussing topics related to personal growth, psychology, and inner child work.

Affirmations

Affirmations can be powerful tools to promote positivity and connect with the inner child. Here's a list of 50 affirmations tailored to foster a positive and nurturing relationship with one's inner child:

1. I am deserving of love and happiness.

2. My inner child is a valuable part of who I am.

3. I embrace the innocence and joy within my inner child.

4. I am safe, and I can trust the journey of life.

5. Every day, I am growing and healing.

6. I release the need to be perfect; I am perfectly me.

7. It's okay to express my feelings and needs.

8. I am resilient, and I can overcome any challenges.

9. My inner child is worthy of kindness and compassion.

THE INNER CHILD AND RELATIONSHIPS

10. I am surrounded by love and support.

11. I choose to let go of past hurts and embrace a brighter future.

12. I am free to play, have fun, and enjoy life.

13. Each day brings new opportunities for happiness and fulfillment.

14. My inner child deserves respect and understanding.

15. I am proud of the progress I've made in my healing journey.

16. I choose to forgive and release negativity from my past.

17. I honor and cherish the child within me.

18. I trust the wisdom of my inner child to guide me.

19. My inner child is a source of creativity and inspiration.

20. I am capable of creating a life filled with love and joy.

21. I lovingly nurture the child within me with positive thoughts.

22. My inner child is a beacon of light, guiding me toward happiness.

23. I am worthy of all the good things life has to offer.

24. My heart is open, and I am ready to receive love.

25. I am gentle with myself as I heal and grow.

26. I choose to focus on the present moment and let go of the past.

27. I am a unique and special individual deserving of love.

28. My inner child is a treasure, and I treat them with kindness.

29. I am proud of the person I am becoming.

30. I release self-doubt and embrace self-love.

31. I am resilient and capable of handling life's challenges.

32. My inner child is a source of strength and wisdom.

33. I trust the process of life and allow joy to flow into my experience.

34. I am surrounded by positive energy and supportive people.

35. I release all negative beliefs about myself and embrace my worth.

36. My inner child is an essential part of my healing journey.

37. I am a vessel of love and compassion for my inner child.

38. I am deserving of inner peace and serenity.

39. I trust my inner child to lead me toward authenticity.

40. I choose thoughts that nourish and uplift my inner child.

41. I am worthy of love and belonging just as I am.

42. My inner child is a wellspring of creativity and imagination.

43. I am gentle with myself during times of healing and growth.

44. I choose love over fear in every aspect of my life.

45. My inner child is resilient and capable of embracing joy.

46. I am grateful for the lessons my inner child has taught me.

47. I release the need for approval from others; I approve of myself.

THE INNER CHILD AND RELATIONSHIPS

48. I am a source of love and comfort for my inner child.

49. My inner child is a cherished part of my being, deserving of care.

50. I am on a journey of self-discovery, and I am proud of my progress.

51. I am deserving of love and acceptance just as I am.

52. My inner child is a source of strength, wisdom, and resilience.

53. I release the past and embrace the positive changes unfolding within me.

54. I nurture my inner child with kindness and compassion.

55. Every positive change I make today honors my inner child's journey.

56. I am open to healing, and positive transformation is happening within me.

57. I trust the process of growth and change in my inner child.

58. I am worthy of all the love and joy life has to offer.

59. My inner child is a beacon of creativity and inspiration.

60. I release old patterns that no longer serve me, making space for positive change.

61. I am committed to creating a safe and nurturing environment for my inner child.

62. Positive change begins with self-love, and I am worthy of that love.

63. I embrace the power of forgiveness to heal my inner child.

64. I am free to create a joyful and fulfilling life for my inner child.

65. Every step I take toward positive change empowers my inner child.

66. I am in control of my thoughts and choose positivity.

67. My inner child is a cherished part of who I am, and I treat them with love.

68. I release the need for perfection and embrace the journey of self-discovery.

69. I am a vessel of love, and that love radiates to my inner child.

70. Positive change is a natural and beautiful part of my inner child's growth.

71. I celebrate the uniqueness and authenticity of my inner child.

72. I am resilient, and my inner child is resilient too.

73. Each day brings new opportunities for positive change and growth.

74. My inner child deserves to experience the joy of living fully.

75. I am patient with myself as I navigate the process of positive change.

76. I release fear and doubt, embracing the courage within my inner child.

77. I trust the journey of my inner child, knowing it leads to positive transformation.

THE INNER CHILD AND RELATIONSHIPS

78. My inner child is a source of boundless creativity and imagination.

79. I am surrounded by love, and my inner child feels that love deeply.

80. Positive change is a beautiful reflection of the love I have for my inner child.

81. I am a loving guardian of my inner child, guiding them with kindness.

82. My inner child is safe, loved, and free to express themselves.

83. I release the weight of the past, allowing my inner child to soar with positivity.

84. I am attuned to the needs and desires of my inner child.

85. My inner child is an integral part of my whole and complete self.

86. I honor my inner child's emotions and allow them to flow freely.

87. Positive change is a testament to the strength and resilience within my inner child.

88. I am grateful for the lessons my inner child teaches me daily.

89. My inner child deserves a life filled with love, joy, and abundance.

90. Positive change is a gift I give to myself and my inner child.

91. I am a beacon of positivity, inspiring my inner child to thrive.

92. I am open to learning and growing alongside my inner child.

93. My inner child's laughter and joy bring light to every aspect of my life.

94. I trust the unfolding of my inner child's journey toward positive change.

95. Every breath I take nurtures and supports my inner child's well-being.

96. I am a loving guide, leading my inner child towards positive transformation.

97. My inner child is a reflection of the love and care I provide them.

98. Positive change is a continuous, beautiful journey within my inner child.

99. I release self-doubt and embrace the boundless potential within my inner child.

100. My inner child is worthy of all the love, joy, and positive changes life has to offer.

Conclusion

In these pages, light was shed on the wounded parts of ourselves we all carry - the inner child frozen in time, holding onto pain from ages ago. With gentleness and empathy, these tender places were embraced. The message was sent that it was finally safe to come out into the open and receive the love they always deserved.

This work requires tremendous vulnerability, yet the rewards are life-changing. By integrating forgotten aspects of ourselves, we become whole. Our relationships deepen from superficial to soulful. We break free of limiting patterns passed down through generations. Most importantly, we cultivate radical self-love and acceptance exactly as we are.

Hopefully you now feel empowered, knowing you have all the wisdom within already to nurture your inner child consistently.

No matter how wounded the past, one's essence remains pristine, innocent, and perfect beyond measure. We need only let go of old stories and see through the lens of compassion to reveal the beauty waiting to be unlocked. Suffering arises from believing ourselves flawed or deficient. But on a core level, we are sacred exactly as we are, worthy of unconditional love.

This journey requires dedication and courage every step of the way. There will be resistance, setbacks, and uncertainty. But much progress has already been made. And the light kindled inside serves as a beacon guiding us through the darkest nights of the soul. We know now where to seek shelter in any storm.

In receiving this gift ourselves, we become a healing presence for others. The world needs our hard-won wisdom. Our empathy makes space for people's pain without judgment. We ignite hope in those still trapped, reliving their past wounds. Our example invites them to walk a new path, just as so many journeyed with us.

It's so important to break dysfunctional patterns handed down through generations. The cycles of abuse, addiction, and neglect end with us. Our commitment to meet the inner child with radical gentleness shifts everything. The impact ripples across time. Our descendants will inherit new legacies of self-awareness, conscious relating, and emotional resilience instead of buried trauma.

To your success!

www.ingramcontent.com/pod-product-compliance
Lightning Source LLC
LaVergne TN
LVHW021829060526
838201LV00058B/3571